ELEVATE YOUR SOUL

BY

ROBIN RAGHOONANDUN

ZORBA BOOKS

ZORBA BOOKS

Published by Zorba Books, August 2024
Website: www.zorbabooks.com
Email: info@zorbabooks.com
Author Name: Robin Raghoonandun
Copyright ©: Robin Raghoonandun

Title: Elevate Your Soul

Printbook ISBN: 978-93-5896-575-9
Ebook ISBN: 978-93-5896-904-7

Zorba Books Pvt. Ltd. (opc)
Sushant Arcade,
Next to Courtyard Marriot,
Sushant Lok 1, Gurgaon – 122009, India

Printed by Manipal Technologies Limited
A1 & A2 Shivalli Industrial Area Manipal Udupi, Karnataka – 57610

DEDICATION

This book is dedicated to

Sri Sri Paramahansa Yogananda
The Ascended Masters of the Universe
All Guardian Angels
My daughter Neha

Contents

❖   *Contents*   ❖

Preface

Robin Raghoonandun, Grand Master of Reiki and spiritual guide, lives in Mauritius, Indian Ocean. Nowadays, he is also known as Guruji by his followers. His parents are late Sohundee Raghoonandun & Ganoomuttee Gunesh. He lost his father at the age of seven.

He studied brilliantly at Royal College Curepipe and the University of Mauritius. He holds a BTech (Hons) in Mechanical Engineering & a Masters in Business Administration. His career was rich with managerial & senior managerial positions in the private sector & he left employment definitely in 2014 to start social work. But what mostly interested him was the paranormal world and meditation which he started at the age of twenty-one.

His life was certainly influenced by the numerous religious persons & teachers he met during his life & who tried their best to answer his questions but the one man who definitely guided him on the path was his revered Spiritual Master Sri Sri Paramahansa Yogananda.

During those ten years of social work, he has healed many persons from complex, sometimes incurable diseases, initiated people in Reiki healing and meditation, gave yoga classes, and spiritual speeches and started charity with volunteers to children, handicapped persons & the homeless. Now, he has started to share Universal Knowledge with all those who are willing to grow spiritually.

He also has a personal blog, www.enlightenfast.com where he writes regularly on spiritual matters & the situation in the world.

Sri Sri Paramahansa Yogananda

Chapter 1

The Soul, Body & Mind

The soul is that spiritual spark which keeps the body alive. It is a tiny part of the Eternal Light of God.

In the course of creation, the Almighty God impregnated all bodies with a part of His energy to give birth to life. He enters all living bodies as breath and fire, and He dwells in the heart of all living beings as a silent observer. We name the God who lives in us as the soul. This is the religious & spiritual explanation of life. Until today, the science which rules this material world has been unable to give a rational explanation of life. But science does agree with the spiritual texts that there was indeed a Big Bang at the time of creation. This information was already available in religious texts more than five thousand years ago. Probably science will need more time to agree with the religious & spiritual texts.

The soul is atomic, that is, it is invisible to the naked eye & even to the most powerful microscope. The mystery around life is the answer to the question: what is it that leaves the body at the time of death which makes it inanimate? If we are doubtful about

> **The reason is that God hides many of the secrets of creation from man. But these secrets become available to those who want to search for them. And the search is a spiritual search, not a scientific search.**

the nature & immense power of the soul, I would like you to think for a minute about the power & minuteness of an atomic bomb.

Hasn't mankind tapped the immense energy of nuclear atoms to manufacture & use a nuclear bomb in Hiroshima? Haven't we witnessed its huge power based on a few kilograms only? Then, why is it difficult to accept that a tiny soul can make a body perform all its complex activities? Furthermore, if human intelligence can develop so many sophisticated technologies, then who is that intelligence that has created the greatly sophisticated Universe? It certainly did not happen by chance as it is logical there must be a higher intelligence at work in the Universe that is sustaining life. But the scientific ego is not ready to accept "**someone**" more capable & more intelligent than itself. This is where the drama lies. Science is based on proofs & experiments whereas spirituality is based on faith. I will add that science is the study of secondary causes whereas wisdom is the study of primary causes. Gradually, science is starting to believe in spiritual knowledge, thanks to the hard work of many elevated spiritual masters who are feeding the scientific world with knowledge of the Universe.

The function of the soul is to send vital energy to the different energy centres or chakras inside our body. In turn, these chakras provide the necessary metabolic energy to that part of the body where they are situated. The soul is divine energy. Energy can neither be created nor destroyed but simply transformed into other forms of energy. Now, God is said to be unborn, originally existed, will never die & can take any form. Do you note the huge similarity between energy & God? God also has no body & shape and is thought of as an infinite reservoir of love & light. What is love & light? They are both states of energy. And when we go back Home to where we originally belonged, there is a beautiful merging of the individual soul or individual energy with the Highest soul or Highest energy, that is God. Of this, I am

100% sure because this is what is written in the oldest religious & spiritual book available called the Vedas. This is what is going to happen to all souls at the time of the dissolution of this whole Universe. And this timing is a divine timing only known to God & His serious followers. And since we are in 2024, I will say that there are roughly 427,000 years to go before the end of the world. This is what Lord Krishna informs Arjuna in the Bhagavad Gita (chapter 8:17). The explanation is that in Hinduism, it is believed that life is categorized into four ages: Satya, Dwapar, Treta & Kaliyuga which repeat in cycles. And each cycle has its own duration- we are currently in the Kaliyuga, which started some five thousand years ago. The total duration of Kaliyuga is 432,000 years, meaning we have 427,000 years to go. After the Kaliyuga is over, the cycle repeats itself starting with Satya, which is a completely pure age where evil does not exist.

The soul is feminine by nature. When she is firmly attached to the five senses by serving them, then she is lost & is not even aware of her true nature. She is forced into the region of the changeable & is confused. When she is made aware of her real identity, then she moves to the other world, the region of eternal life, where she finds her freedom. That state of the soul, when she has stopped being a slave to the senses of the body, is described as wisdom. To simplify the explanation of soul & body, just imagine the battery of a car that supplies electric energy to the lights, music player, on-board computer, Bluetooth, etc. It is the same scenario with the soul. For someone who does not know how a car functions, that person will be bewildered by the different functions of the car. But for somebody who knows about the functions of a battery inside the body of the car, then for that person, there is absolutely no mystery. In the beginning, science taught us about atoms & molecules being the indivisible smallest representative of all matter- this is basic chemistry taught to secondary college students. But what has happened today? That same science has discovered that atoms are made up of other smaller particles! So, you see, science is sometimes not reliable but is the driving force of the material world- it makes us believe things and then, after some more research, it changes its version of the truth with new findings. Then, this means the original findings were not the truth!

The soul records all our activities & experiences to determine our next birth- this is the way it works. Our soul is intelligent enough to grant us the kind of life that we want unconsciously. I have used the term unconscious because we are not aware that the kind of life that we live is a message we are sending to the Universe- the message that this is the way we are happy. And what the Universe concludes is that we have this preference (or not because it can be unconscious too!), so we come back to enjoy the same kind of life. Suppose someone spends his life doing business, then the chances of coming back to do business are very high because this is what is recorded in the soul. If a person enjoys a married life, then marriage shall be present in the next life. And if one says I am fed up with a human life, then the chances of not getting born again are also high. But the sad truth is very few of us are aware of this very important Universal Knowledge & we go through life without knowing, we die without knowing & we come back again on Earth with all our ignorance packed inside of us & the cycle repeats- until one day, in one birth, our ignorance is illuminated by the light of superior knowledge! That is when awakening happens and of course, we shall not remember what we did in our previous lives, but a paradigm shift in the consciousness will have started. Now, the spiritual awareness becomes stronger & the Path becomes available to tread on.

I have stated earlier that the soul records all our activities & experiences. This knowledge has two beautiful implications which the serious spiritual aspirant must understand. The first one is that at the time of creation, the soul is new & bare just like a brand-new USB key. And you will recall that the soul is a tiny part of the Eternal light of God. Therefore, this is the original state of the soul. Now, that soul is assigned a human body & is sent to Earth or other material planets which exist in the Universe. But let us focus on Earth only. As soon as this soul starts living, recording of activities & experiences will start. The body will die, the soul will take another human form & will be born again. More recording will ensue to sustain repeated births & deaths. The second implication is what happens if a spiritual aspirant receives the Universal Knowledge that the soul can be cleansed & be made new again just like we delete the files on a USB key? Then having been cleansed of all knowledge, experiences, activities & all that the soul has been through in all lives, the soul becomes bare & barren once again & goes back Home to the source of all creations, that is God. So how is soul cleansing done? Verily, there is no spiritual practice for that & it happens uniquely by the Grace of God. But we can promote its happening by living a spiritual life seriously & wait & pray that the God of Salvation effectively salvages our soul. It is based on spiritual meritocracy. If we deserve it, by great hard work, then we shall surely get it. At this stage, it will be the end of physical life & the start of a purely spiritual life.

Souls can be described as old or young. If a soul has been repeatedly coming to Earth through many births & deaths, then that soul is an old soul. We recognize an old soul by its behaviour in the body; people with old souls will find great difficulty in adapting to the modern world & its new fashions. They will prefer the old style in everything be it music, films, way of dressing, eating, etc. They will also have greater wisdom in solving the problems of life but at the same time, they shall also be the ones who will be suffering the most. They will tend to be misunderstood by most people & they can stir a lot of jealousy around them for nothing, only by being truly who they are. But in the end, they are the ones who are right! Old souls tend to be very intelligent & they have the capacity to understand others readily. All this means that an old soul is very near its final stage of salvation & it has to turn its life more inwards rather than struggle every day with the mundane world. Turning inwards means adopting a spiritual way of life, meditating, practicing yoga & charity towards the needy & poor. On the contrary, young souls find they fit well in the modern world & have absolutely no complaints to make. They are in the right place & they do their best to take advantage of all the benefits that the modern world provides them with. They have little or no religious/ or spiritual activities & are most suited to enjoy life.

The soul is encapsulated in the body, in the middle of the chest- more precisely in a secret chamber inside the heart chakra. We are living due to the presence of God inside of us. Our body is mortal in that it is made of physical matter. But our soul is eternal just like the God who created us. All this is confirmed & agreed upon by all major religions. The human body has often been described as more sophisticated than the most advanced computer ever designed. And scientists are spending millions of dollars trying to replicate the work of God. But they are using available materials such as cells for replication whereas the original creation was the transformation of energy into physical matter.

The body is made up also of energy centres and energy canals which flow inside of us, interconnecting all the centres together. We also have electricity in our body to make our brain & the central nervous system operate as well as to make the heart pump blood to all our cells. Did you know that the heart has a natural "**battery**" which gets recharged by exposure to the Sun rays? My Gurudev (spiritual master) informed the world to stay in the morning sunlight for ten minutes every day to keep this natural battery fully charged & to get positive hormones in the body. And what is the modern world doing to us? It is confining us in the comforts of a house or an office- it is therefore making us move away from our true nature. Just imagine how you feel after a trip to the seaside, waterfall, lakeside, forest or mountain. This feeling is because our true identity belongs to the nature that surrounds us, not the material environment that we have created. I feel suffocated if I don't go out in nature a few times per week. This is my personal experience. And when I miss the contact, my body reacts & signals me I have missed something very important & I just leave everything aside to go somewhere in nature! As an experiment, in Summer, try to get drenched for a few minutes in the rain in your yard one day- you will be astonished by the results.

The human body is made up of thoughts- my spiritual master says it is exactly thirty-five thoughts. What are thoughts? They are packets of energy emitted by the mind. It has also been proven by science that thoughts & intelligence are electromagnetic. Our eternal God, being the Cosmic Mind, has the power to transform energy into matter- this is apparently being observed in space now by powerful telescopes. And the reverse process also is possible, that is, the conversion of matter into energy- this is the principle of action of a bomb, isn't it? The material of the bomb disintegrates into finer particles & hot gas. But these can also be further reduced to more subtle states, which is not possible by science today. That is when matter turns back into thoughts again. If the idea of physical matter being made of thoughts & energy does not appeal to you, let us examine the job of engineers & architects. What they are doing is thinking, designing & then building. But the basic function is to think first; this is exactly what the eternal God did before giving us the Universe. God thought about all the details, then through his creative divine power, created everything in this Universe. There must be an intelligence & a thinker who has performed all this creation. And the human being created in the image of God, certainly also has creative power but at a human level - this is logical when we look around at all the objects we have created.

The human body possesses consciousness through its five senses of sight, hearing, smell, taste & touch. However, it has been proven by many elevated souls that we can develop superconsciousness like healing energy, clairaudience, clairvoyance, prediction of the future, reading of thoughts, astral projections & many others. All these are not magical powers but capacities which are dormant inside of us & which can be accessed by spiritual techniques. The modern person will certainly doubt these human faculties but if we consider that science has proven that we are using only 9% of our brain capacity, viz, intelligence, then the question which arises is: What are we capable of when we increase the usage of the brain power to 15%, 20% & so on? What happens at 100% of utilisation?

On the other hand, I can guarantee you that a fully spiritual person can perform tasks that an ordinary man cannot do. I recall a spectacular healing which I did on a three-year-old girl in 2022. She fainted in the schoolyard & from there, she stopped talking, was suffering from fits on & off & was very reluctant to eat. Her parents tried all kinds of treatment until they came to see me as a last resort. There she was, a lovely girl with green eyes, who always stared at me right in my eyes all the time as if she was reading my mind or knew who I was. And I started her treatment- she began

speaking after a few sessions. Then, they all flew to India for some further tests & treatment. She came to visit me with her parents after several weeks, and fully recovered. This time, when I knelt down to talk to her, she immediately left the lap of her father, came towards me & hugged me! I melted. I will never forget that moment. They offered me a small white Ganesha statue, which is still on the dashboard of my car. As it happens, the potential of a human being is huge but we remain stuck as a mere mortal because either we don't believe or we have not been exposed to such events. In any way, we have to find out who we really are & we are certainly not that mortal body that we see in the mirror- this is a great illusion!

The human being is also made up of a mind which is basically the essence of our existence. The mind can also be termed as spirit. Spirit animates the body with its divine power, which is electromagnetic in nature. There is not a proper seat of the mind in the body- it is simply found everywhere all around our body. We can view the mind as an electromagnetic version of the body, with exactly the same shape. Some people state that the mind is also in the heart. The mind is very powerful & is the creative & conscious part of our body. We are what our mind is- this common saying is so true. When we are awake, we are essentially using the body but when we are sleeping & dreaming, then we are mostly spirit.

The mind has a consciousness of its own & can take control of our nature. It can make us do things that are against our will & which are not normal. This happens when the mind has lost its purity & is conditioned by negativities. The conditioned mind will make a person deviate from the normal & righteous procedures of life. So, what are these negativities which can pollute the mind just like viruses & malware which affect a computer? They are essentially our negative thoughts. And these negative thoughts after being generated by the mind, affect bodily functions via diseases. Negative thoughts can go a long way to cause major disruptions in our physical, emotional & mental wellbeing. The contrary also happens in the sense that physical, emotional & mental imbalances also affect the mind adversely.

Control of the mind is therefore of utmost importance to live a balanced life. In all human activities, there are only three possibilities that exist: either these activities are of the right dose, of excess dose or limited dose. This simple truth applies to eating, drinking, sleeping, exercising, resting, watching television, praying, meditating, going out, gardening, staying on the internet, playing games, etc. Behind all our activities, it is the mind which has "**decided**" to do them, right? Therefore, when we become conscious that we are either overdoing or depriving ourselves, then only can we correct the situation & come back to equilibrium. In order to achieve this, the mind must undergo training. That training will make the mind work for us rather than work against us because both can happen. The training consists of developing mindfulness. It is like a radar which is constantly scanning all our activities & which asks the same question each time: am I in the deprivation zone, in the exaggeration zone or in the balanced zone? This is called the taming of the mind. Because the nature of the mind is restless & fickle if left on its own without control. And the mind does not know how to discriminate between right & wrong - it is the intelligence that has this responsibility. An intelligent person has sufficient knowledge in all areas of his life & is thus guided. At advanced stages of personal development, the need to rely on intelligence shall not arise as it is intuition which shall be the driving force. Intuition is knowing without really knowing- we just feel in our entire being that this decision is the one we must take. Intuition is a quality which can be developed by meditation & staying calm all the time.

Research in American & European institutes has shown that the majority of time, the mind is in a negative mode. This is a surprising fact and yet it is the conclusion of the study of thousands of people to determine their mode of thinking. It was found that 80% of the time, the research group was thinking negatively. And sadly, this is what is happening across the world because we have not been taught about the functioning of the mind. If we analyse our life, we shall effectively see that we are very often thinking of worst-case scenarios rather than optimistic results. The reason for this is that we are all worried!

But few people are aware of this condition: the student worries about failing examinations or not pleasing the parents, the employee is worried about the manager's reactions, the drivers are worried about traffic jams, the married couple is worried if they are going to get children or divorce one day, the lovers worry if their partners are cheating on them, youngsters worry about their social media, etc. To stop worrying is a central pillar of spiritual practice. Again, it is our mind which makes us decide whether we shall worry or not, isn't

> *Worry is at the centre of our lives & is deeply rooted inside of us.*

it? But we always decide to do negative things with our mind & that is why we suffer.

Spiritually, it is said that the realisation of the Higher Self is the rectification of the mind.

You will note here that this spiritual instruction is not referring to meditation, renunciation, asceticism, practicing rituals, fasting, pilgrimage to sacred temples or places, visiting the birthplace of saints & yogis, visiting temples every week, etc. The main focus of enlightenment is the correction of our mind. Why is that? Simply because with our mind, we think & we act. Our actions are linked to our karma- that is we reap what we sow. I am most grateful to the great sages who have passed on this knowledge to me & I am sharing it with you so that you reflect on it. It will not be easy to start acting on it as when I learnt about it myself, it took me a while before I started implementing it. And what a release! It is so simple. So, behaviour is more important than anything else- that is the lesson that you must retain. At all times, our behaviour must be in line with the divine world. That is all that God wants from us as He is not impressed by our ritualistic offerings but by the purity of our intention, our sacrifices and our love for Him. I have heard about & witnessed people fighting & arguing loudly in temples or even making devotees cry with harsh language. Then what is the use of praying? Are we blessed by such behaviour or do we fall down? When our mind & heart are pure, then only pure behaviour will follow & it is certainly not by going to temples, churches & mosques that the cleansing shall be achieved. It is only dedicated hard work on the mind & heart which will give the required help. And when God sees that you are willing to change, then He will help you. I will also inform you that it is conduct & behaviour which is the cause of reborn-ness on Earth.

Chapter 2

The Methods to Transform Our Inner Energy

> *When a person has become truly calm, then he will understand the Great Laws of the Universe.*
> *(Chinese Proverb)*

Our energy is personal to us & we are responsible for its use, preservation & management. Nobody informs us of this fantastic piece of information; we live only in the consciousness & the caring of the body. The entire transformation of our internal energy is a process or a journey full of experience & learning. The start of the process can be at any age and the journey will still be very interesting & it will take its own time. As a matter of fact, every individual has his frequency of vibration & a corresponding degree of evolution. It is impossible to hasten things & to take control of the process as it is the divine world which operates at its pace. Sometimes, it is stated that such an event happens only when God himself chooses the person He wishes to grant those spiritual aspects - also known as the Grace of God.

Very often, the choice of a spiritual life happens after a great emotional shock like the loss of a dear one, a divorce, a major personal accident, a near-death experience (NDE) and a severe medical condition. The common aspect in all these conditions is that the individual undergoes a great imbalance of personal energy. And it is that very imbalance which is a trigger to think of getting on the Path of self-realisation. At other times, when the ego is hurt badly, the same phenomenon can be observed. When you start to think & feel that nothing is valuable on this Earth, when you sink in total darkness & despair, then a shift occurs whereby you decide to travel on an unknown road- the spiritual road. That is the beginning of the first steps on the spiritual Path. It is said that the greatness of happiness can be valued only when you taste the sour experience of great unhappiness & sorrow, just like it is a person who has crossed a desert for several days who knows the value of a glass of water. All these are the unconventional ways of treading on the spiritual Path.

A very rare instance happens when an individual is born with a spiritually pre-determined mission like Lord Krishna & Lord Jesus. In Hinduism, this phenomenon is said to happen every millennium, whereby an Avatar is born. An Avatar is God Himself, who takes a human form to come & solve the dire conditions in which human beings are living due to their irresponsible actions. This usually happens when life on Earth becomes reckless to a point that only the divine intervention can assist. Great spiritual masters & saints can get reborn to complete the tasks of their previous births or simply, they have wished to come back to help mankind. All our solutions lie in the divine realm but the human race is so badly blindfolded that it believes that material solutions are the only ones available at hand. It is only after an astounding deal of earthly turmoil that orderliness is achieved again. Nature operates in cycles just like the seasons; there are definitely cycles of peace & turmoil. We are actually in a phase of acute imbalance which will end to yield to a period of peace.

Then, there exists a myriad of techniques which can kickstart a deep search for the unknown or the treading on the Path. Usually, a religious person, that is, one who believes in God and who practices religious rituals regularly can be a potential spiritual aspirant. However, it is not the only condition that needs to be satisfied. Religion in itself cannot answer the deep inquisitiveness of a serious spiritual aspirant. So, inquisitiveness is one condition that is required; the more one starts questioning life, the more the chances of becoming spiritual. I started questioning at the age of seven after my father passed away.

Spirituality and religion are two completely different divine phenomena & should not be mixed. A religious person can be "**blocked**" in his religious practices for a whole lifetime without knowing that there is a higher aspect of himself, which he is neglecting. This is called ignorance. Religion is based on emotions & a socio-cultural identity whereas spirituality is based on the proper use of  the mind & the transformation of the person. A religious person can increase his religious character by getting more involved & by looking for more information, like studying a sacred religious book like the Bhagavad Gita, the Bible or the Quran.

In this way, the amount of knowledge will gradually start to take over the ignorance of the individual. Spiritually, this is called the overcoming of the darkness of ignorance with the light of knowledge. The fire of spiritual knowledge or Universal Knowledge is indeed fabulous as it illuminates the dark side of the person - this is the start of the journey towards enlightenment. Of course, the study should be continued & not be just a mere curiosity to read. Emphasis must be laid on study. When we bear in mind that the God who is inside

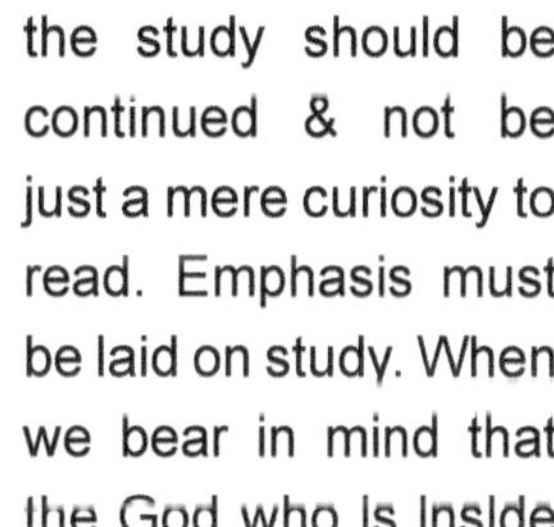

of us is observing what we do, then obviously we are rewarded for our actions & thus progress is ensured. The most important part of studying religion & spirituality is the implementation phase. This is exactly where most spiritual aspirants fail & abandon the Path. The task at hand is not a simple one but the rewards are great.

Another way of becoming spiritual is to start meditation. There are many techniques of meditation & you can choose any one with which you feel comfortable. The point is to start without much thinking about the results. Eventually, everything will settle in its place in due time. Meditation is an act of controlling our thoughts to experience a state of deep calmness. Our thoughts come from our mind; therefore, we are controlling our mind with the help of meditation. At another level, to meditate means to go deeper inside of us to find the Truth. The concentration on energy points in the body, like the third eye or the heart chakra greatly increases the inner power & the personal frequency of vibration of the practitioner. In parallel, the act of meditation also expands the consciousness. Fifteen minutes of meditation twice a day is a good start, with one session early morning before sunrise & another session before going to sleep. Care should be exercised not to overdo things because there are great chances of getting carried away by the magnificence of the spiritual energy. Fifteen minutes of meditation seem at first to be simple but I can assure you that waking up before sunrise is a feat that few of us are capable of achieving because laziness & the comfort of a bed will be stronger than your willpower to start meditation. But, with perseverance, the objective shall be reached & with time, you shall not even need an alarm clock to wake up -it will be automatic. At this stage, it is worthwhile to note that the divine world, wherever it is in parallel dimensions & galaxies to us, wakes up at three in the morning every day. If you observe that you are regularly opening your eyes from sleep at this particular time, then the chances of you being a spiritual person are very high!

Next, yoga postures are also very helpful when deciding to walk on the spiritual Path. Yoga is a Sanskrit word which means union with the divine. Therefore, any devotional practice like prayer, worship, singing and meditation are all forms of yoga. The most helpful posture of yoga is called padmasana or lotus posture & is the best sitting posture for deep meditation. There are in all eighty-four yoga postures & the main purpose is to rejuvenate the body, mind & soul. Several yoga postures act directly on the raising of the Kundalini  from the base of the spine up to the third eye & crown chakras, e.g. the mountain posture. Kundalini is viewed as a serpentine energy which is closely related to spiritual awakening & which transforms the inner energy of a person. This transformation is what is required to get access to enlightenment.

It is acclaimed that the practice of yoga postures is greatly beneficial for health & suppleness. If a yoga practitioner has sufficient experience in yoga postures & can stay in one posture for two & a half hours, then the inner transformation is huge. Now, very few people will try to go to this limit but this is what is required- pushing our limits safely to discover our enormous potential!

Besides yoga, Reiki initiation is also recommended to start getting experiences with energy. Reiki is a Japanese form of natural healing which uses the chakra in the palm hand to channel divine healing to oneself or others. The Reiki practitioner never uses his /her personal energy to heal but instead, the divine energy flows from its source through the body and out of the palm chakras. The palm chakras are found in the middle of each palm. Chakras are centres of energy in our body, which control the proper functioning of all the organs situated around them - there are over a hundred chakras in the human body & there are seven main chakras located along the spinal column from the coccyx to the top of the skull. To get access to the Reiki energy, one has to be initiated by a Reiki Master, who will perform the initiation of the first level. There are five levels in all, the fifth level being the Grand Master level.

Each initiation is a wonderful experience, whereby one immediately feels a change in one's energy. During the initiation, several unimaginable experiences may be possible like: visions of beautiful auric colours, seeing animals, smelling fragrances you have never encountered before, visions of ancestors, tremors in the body, sudden crying, vibration in specific chakras, cold or hot currents in the body & many more. Once you are initiated, you have Reiki in your hands for your whole life & from there, you can start a process of self-healing from diseases as well as the regular cleansing of the seven main chakras from heavy, dense negative energies. When your chakras are in good health & are free from negative energies, you have a high state of energy & your frequency of vibration is raised. Therefore, if you practice Reiki regularly, your energy will be higher than a normal person. And gradually, this energy will increase & spiritual experiences will start to appear. This enhances the faith of the person in the divine & it can be stipulated that the spiritual journey on the Path has already started. Reiki opens up the world of energy to the practitioner & energy is everything in this Universe. Energy is superior to matter & the highest form of energy is the Creator of All That Is. But again, regularity & self-discipline are mandatory - I see so many people whom I have initiated who do not practice regularly and still, they wait for a major transformation in their health or lives.

Recitation of mantras using a mala or any string of beads is also a powerful technique to get access to the spiritual world & to perform the transformation of energy. Mantras when recited daily at specific times release packets of energy which get absorbed by the practitioner. Sound is energy & a mantra is a sacred sound which helps to connect with that Deity to whom you are praying. It is worth mentioning that before all Creation, there was total emptiness as well as a specific humming sound close to that made by bees. This is called the sound of the Universe & is the last resonance of the word Aum - it is like stretching the letter 'm' for several seconds. Therefore, mantra recitation will help get closer to the divine world. I have students who have reported being completely lost by long recitation of mantras, just like in a meditative state. However, as with any spiritual practice, regularity & long duration are crucial; this is where many people quit because they do not find the required time or they are unable to cut down television views or other material activities to devote to spiritual practices. If you are unable to say no to a late-night invitation or are too tired to practice after a late-night event, then there shall be little progress. There might even be abandoning of the spiritual search. Patience is definitely paramount when walking on the Path.

All the various ways I have explained so far, i.e. meditation, yoga, Reiki & mantra recitation deal with enhancing the inner energy of the person. A great level of transformation will be clearly perceived but this is not the maximum potential that can be developed. And this is exactly

what I thought as I was already doing many extraordinary healings with the energy level that I had reached. So, I decided to plunge even deeper to see what was possible. The next steps, coupled with the previous ones will embark the spiritual aspirant on the highest possible level.

So, what are these new steps? Broadly speaking, the spiritual seeker will now have to start a process of transforming his/her character & behaviour. As weird and irrational as this may seem, a proper character is essential in the pursuit of higher development. This is the domain of morality, the purging of all negativities inside of us. In a nutshell, a series of soft skills must be cultivated: patience, perseverance, kindness, gentleness, humility, resilience, trust, honesty, avoidance of restlessness, no reaction to the flames of emotions, non sensuality, stopping having regrets from the past, not worrying at all about the future, integrity, wisdom, allowing life to guide you, remaining calm all the time, taking things as they come, avoiding pride, lust, anger & ostentation. Now, this seems a lot to do & many of you will say *"Oh, that's not for me."* But a stepwise & disciplined approach will surely help you. And it is not a mistake if you fail in the beginning because failure also is crucial in self-realisation – you have to fail repeatedly & feel bad to start over again. And this can happen several times until at last, success is yours. It is not a rule to have it the first time & that you cannot try again as if it is just an examination with age restrictions & number of limited attempts. That is not the way it works! As long as you are serious & determined & you really know what you are aiming at, it shall be yours in divine timing. When you are able to reach that highest stage, it is the end of all suffering.

Before ending this chapter, I feel I must share another vital spiritual knowledge with you. It is another spiritual practice that must be developed, which is linked with our consciousness.

When we grow up, it happens in phases. And then, we reach adulthood. In this process, when we are an adult, many of us adopt the attitude that it is immature to behave as a child. This is a serious mistake! I have learnt with time & experience plus I have also been guided by the divine world to develop the child's consciousness. Childishness & childlikeness are not the same stuff. It is the latter that one must develop. So, who is a child? That is the question. A child is the one whom God prefers to adults. And this truth is so destabilising, isn't it? In my country, there is a song the title of which is "*In children, there is God.*" I firmly believe that all around the world, in all cultures, the same belief is firmly held. And what a marvellous piece of Universal Knowledge! The child is innocent, has purity of heart, is open, doesn't worry, is harmless, lives in the moment, trusts that his/her parents will take good care of him/her, is willing to learn & is playful. Just imagine how many adults you can detect in the child's state. Very few. And this is what one must practice. Carl Jung, the father of psychology has studied this particular aspect of a child compared to an adult & I had the opportunity to read his report on the matter. I was shocked that his scientific discovery was in total alignment with a spiritual truth. In fact, Carl Jung found that all of our problems could be solved if we could make that child consciousness be borne again in our adult minds. God is simply great. In the Bible, Lord Jesus states: "*Truly I tell you, unless you change & become like children, you shall never enter the Kingdom of God.*" (Matthew 18:3)

Chapter 3

The Power of Positive Thinking

> *We are what our mind is. Our mind is our best friend &*
> *worst enemy. (Lord Krishna)*

Most of us have surely heard about the saying: "*Be positive, think positive & act positive.*" But until we start delving into the spiritual world, we shall not grasp its deep essence. In truth, a positive core is the building block of self-realisation. Being positive all the time is not an easy task & we especially need to remain positive even when the whole world around us is tumbling down! That is the real test of a spiritual aspirant & it requires a phenomenal amount of mental power to keep going, even when life is treating us unkindly. So, to be positive is an instruction to the spiritual seekers. And there is absolutely no alternative.

To become a positive human antenna & to radiate love & light all around, you will require the careful & disciplined training of the mind. Spiritually, it is said that the mind is as restless as a monkey. And the more you are stressed or under pressure, the more restless you become. This state causes a great imbalance of the inner energy of the person. The restless person is bound to make mistakes because the mind is fogged by confusion, anger, fear, frustrations & other negative energies. But, when we are conscious that we can intentionally quiet our mind by simply becoming aware that we are restless, fearful, hesitating, worrying

& so on, then only, we can bring ourselves back to equilibrium. Therefore, the most important issue here is to connect with our emotions.

When we are clearly aware of our emotions, then we can know how to act to correct the situation. Now, we have just laid our hands on the biggest dilemma & I would say also the biggest suffering of mankind: the state of being unconscious. Not knowing is a great danger, up to the extent that if one dies in too much unconsciousness, then the chances of taking birth in the animal kingdom are very high! Indeed, we can get out of this trouble by making use of our intelligence to correct our mind. The pace of the modern world does not allow us to rest - we are either constantly thinking or acting till late at night!

In every individual, there is a degree of consciousness as well as a degree of unconsciousness - this inevitably varies from individual to individual. The more the unconsciousness, the more the behaviour is inhuman & animalistic whereas the lesser the unconsciousness, the more divine is human nature. Unconsciousness is directly related to the darkness & negativity of this world. Consciousness is divine light & positivity. From this angle, it is clear that the dangers of unconsciousness are real & certainly not to be underestimated. This is why it is stated that God is all-knowing & an infinite reservoir of love & light. Ignorance of spiritual knowledge makes us deviate from our divine nature & thus, we hurt ourselves & others. Consciousness can be expanded as there is a wide variety of higher levels

of frequencies available. In parallel, learning will decrease unconsciousness & these two processes coupled together put a spiritual aspirant on the Path. Acting on consciousness will help us become more positive - the positive individual understands the great Laws of the Universe and is calm, loving, understanding, compassionate, kind, generous, smiling, forgiving & fearless. All these are spiritual qualities that shall be gifted to the serious student- of this I am 100% sure!

The process of cleansing negativities is called purgation. This is a very important phase in the cultivation of positivity & spiritual advancement. To be able to adopt purgation, we need to know what is impure inside of us, and accept this state of affairs & then change will be possible. Human nature tends to resist changes & fears to move out of its conditioned lifestyle & comfort zones to start walking towards the unknown. To become essentially positive is not an easy task but when we become aware & conscious that we are not living our own lives but only that dictated by our parents, our beliefs & society at large, then this is called waking up! Yes, awakening is the state that we must look for. And when this happens due to an enormous amount of positivity in our lives, then the transformation is complete. A new version of ourselves is born.

Surrendering to God is also an act of building up positivity. Very few people will think about surrendering their lives to God. To voluntarily surrender means that one accepts that one does not know & needs to be trained. Then, it shows a deep sense of humility as well as the acceptance of the existence of our divine parents. Adults tend to forget that they also have a spiritual Father & Mother. And how wonderful it is to have such caring & loving spiritual parents. Our physical parents are quite limited & they are not even aware of it - they believe all the contrary as they are empowered with authority over children, power by their jobs, status as parents & their personal belongings. When we trust God & think that it is great to surrender, then we are effectively asking life to guide us. Lord Jesus stated that He never did things of His own accord but that He abandoned His will to God, making us remember the statement in the Bible: "*Only Thy will shall be done, oh Eternal Father.*" (Matthew 6:10). We shall discover a great power when we allow life to guide us - the power of intuition, that is to do exactly what has to be done in all circumstances.

The problem with physical parents lies in that few parents take the time to teach their children about wisdom & the lessons of life. But do these parents themselves possess wisdom & enough Universal Knowledge to share with their children? Had this been the case, our society would have been in a totally different state today. We don't have the time to think about this, but this is a fundamental flaw in our society- we are performing the upbringing of our children by trial & error. And this is why society has reached the level where it is today. We are getting more & more educated, but we still are not operating at our maximum potential! More important than education are instructions. I studied Mechanical Engineering & I also hold a Master's in Business Administration but these degrees have not helped me in my search for the Truth. And it is only a Spiritual Master who can dictate the required instructions. Now, as the word itself sounds, an instruction is to be obeyed without arguing & seeking explanations- that is the spirit of a humble student who will
make progress.

Many times, when I give instructions to some students, they tell me "**Yes, Guruji, but...**". As soon as you say "**but**", the "**yes**" turns into a "**no.**" It is actually a polite way of disagreeing or it could

be a direct way of challenging authority. But can we disagree with a Spiritual Master?

Being positive means that we are only accepting positive energies to be part of our body. Negative energies are harmful to the delicate tissues of our organs, especially the heart & the brain. We have not been created to entertain negative energies- we are meant to be light, peaceful & wise. And the main advantage of staying positive is that we shall attract only positive persons & things in our life. This is the famous Law of Attraction which is one of the great Laws of the Universe, amongst others.

Truly speaking, we act like robots in our lives; and in difficult situations, we only react. This is because we see everyone around us do this including our parents, teachers, friends & colleagues. It would seem that our intelligence has never been taught that we can choose to remain calm rather than get angry, frustrated or confused. It is worth noting at this point that all diseases start with an imbalance of energy. And it is exactly how those uncontrolled anger, frustrations, confusions, sadness & all other negative energies affect our internal energy.

What is more important for a human being is the internal aspect or energy; whatever is inside, that is exactly what is reflected on the outside. When we are positive, our bloodstream is loaded with positive hormones like serotonin, endorphins & melatonin. And all these positive hormones contribute to our wellbeing & feeling of calm & joy. On the contrary, when there is a high level of negative hormones circulating in our body due to our negative aspect, then we feel bad, irritated & morally down. As you can see, positivity has a tremendous impact on our wellbeing. More than that, I will add that joy, tranquillity & equipoise are all of a chemical nature just like sexual pleasure! This makes sense as 70% of our body is water & blood. There are glands in our body which can secrete chemicals which are helpful for our wellbeing as well as secrete negative hormones such as cortisol which causes illness. I have met patients who were suffering from acid reflux, migraine, insomnia & obesity just because of a high level of cortisol. And these patients were losing so much time & money with medicine & gym subscriptions.

All the symptoms kept persisting for the simple reason that the root cause was stress! And what is stress at its core? It is an imbalance of one's energy caused by a lack of adaptation to the conditions of one's life or a wrong reaction to adverse life conditions such

> **This modern-world suffering,**
> **known as stress,**
> **is the primary cause of 80% of**
> **all known diseases**
> **–it is medically proven.**

as the death of a relative, job loss, changing residence, divorce, financial pressure, job pressure, marital pressure, etc.

I remember when my mother passed away in September 2015, I didn't shed tears at all. My aunts & sisters were pleading with me to stop holding my sorrow & that it was alright to cry. But I was not feeling that sad to burst into tears - this may seem rude but I later realised that the reasons for this were mainly my consciousness which was no longer the same & also because I knew exactly from a standpoint of Universal Knowledge, what happens to dead people. And I had its beautiful confirmation & experience on the eve of the cremation. We were all sitting next to my mother's corpse & all of sudden, when I looked at the door entrance, I saw my mother, father & grandmother looking at me & smiling- they didn't seem unhappy or worried at all. I kept staring at them so much that I didn't even notice that my sister was observing the whole scene. A few days later, she questioned me about the event- I didn't lie to her & she was shocked.

To remain positive twenty-four hours a day is therefore the way of living! The spiritual knowledge of this great procedure of life is that the past is gone, do not dwell on it; about the future, we do not know what will happen; so, what we have is only today! Therefore, the wisdom of this message is to live our life one day at a time rather than harbouring the regrets of the past or being anxious about the events which shall happen in the future. That is the simple way of cultivating a positive attitude to life because the message we are sending to the divine world is that we trust that everything will be fine & that we do not have great sorrows from the past. This procedure or way of living is called the alignment with the spiritual world. Of course, in the beginning, the alignment shall be small & gradually, with perseverance, it will increase until it reaches a point of complete alignment. At this stage, life becomes beautiful as we shall be benefitting from the full support of the spiritual world.

I have been taught by the divine world to become positive in another simple way; this has been instructed by Lord Krishna to Arjuna in the Bhagavad Gita & which was practiced by Lord Krishna himself: it is to smile every day. Smiling to oneself in a mirror and to others on the street, in the bus, at the market place & while watching a movie shows to the divine world that we are at peace with ourselves & with others & also especially at peace with the Universe. It means that we have totally given up complaining. Our loving Father does not like complaints at all. When we complain, it means that we are not developing the quality of being joyful & you will be surprised to learn that God is joy! And how about smiling amidst your personal problems? It is perfectly possible after some practice & that is how Lord Krishna led his life some five thousand years ago. His greatness was such that He smiled although He knew that at any time, a demon could come & threaten His life. He even smiled at the hunter who shot an arrow at His leg while He was resting in the forest. As indicated, there is greatness in smiling & being positive. Therefore, my plea to you is to start today & look for that greatness which is dormant inside of you.

Chapter 4

Solving the Sufferings of Life

> *You are not this body. Your true nature is Spirit. And what is Spirit does not suffer.*

Human suffering is a phenomenon which nobody can escape whether one is rich, poor, educated, uneducated, or even religious. It is only the spiritual person who does not suffer. And I am making this statement out of knowing the truth about suffering & also from personal experience. Suffering can start at an early age during childhood or at later stages in adult life. More precisely, the background of suffering is the possession of a human body. Therefore, the Universal Knowledge applicable here is that whenever we take birth on Earth, then immediately suffering will be part of our life.

On a deeper level, we are born on Earth due to an accumulation of past sins & offenses. And the consequences of such actions are to suffer- this is the basis of human life.

The first cause of suffering is due to ignorance. Ignorance arises because there is a lack of sufficient knowledge in several or all areas of our lives. For example, if we are not aware that excess sugar in our diet & lack of physical exercise will lead to diabetes, then this is an example of a lack of dietary knowledge. If we analyse all our sufferings, we shall see that a good percentage arises due to ignorance. And the most dangerous things will happen to us if we do not look for spiritual knowledge. There is a vast amount of knowledge that is available in the Universe & which is mandatory to gather to live a successful life.

A successful life does not necessarily mean huge wealth & a lot of material possessions. In terms of success, spirituality will help us to be happy, peaceful and kind- hearted. Those are the basic requirements. If one wants to go deeper into the spiritual world, other skills can be developed such as wisdom, patience & psychic skills such as clairvoyance & clairaudience. The danger of ignorance is real & should not be underestimated. But the problem lies in that we do not know that we are ignorant or worse, we believe we are not ignorant. So many times, we hear the sentences "*I know what I am doing*" or "*I have heard about this.*" The question is not about what I know but what I do when I know! It is essentially the implementation which is most important as knowing is necessary but not sufficient. Knowledge without implementation is only entertainment. And the best way to go about learning & implementing is to lead by example- then others will follow.

The next cause of suffering is negligence. Few adults will accept that they are negligent & that is the cause of their sufferings. The reason is because the ego interferes in the process & clouds their intelligence. Negligence is more subtle & dangerous than ignorance. At the level of negligence, we already have the required knowledge that can prevent us from suffering. But what happens is that we persist in the wrong direction despite knowing that it is not the right direction. This is caused by the temptations of the world which are stronger than our willpower.

The mind is either weak or strong; or the mind is under our control or is controlled by other people, by our desires, our greed & our beliefs. I can assure you that all adults can discriminate between good & bad but still, we cannot stop ourselves from committing mistakes & sins. What are the reasons for this? Well, in a nutshell, it is the way we have allowed our life to shape us. We are not conscious of the enormous power that life has to condition us in the way we think & act. That is why it is sometimes stated that phenomenal progress can be achieved by unlearning rather than learning itself! Here, it is specifically our bad habits which are our obstacles. Bad habits can be self-acquired, be family traits passed on from generation to generation, adopted by peer influence, social influence, fashion & sheer unconsciousness.

We also suffer from past life actions & this is called karmic suffering. Karma is real & affects our wellbeing drastically. Isaac Newton, the famous physician discovered a physics law which states that: to every action, there is an equal & opposite reaction. And this is exactly what spirituality teaches us: you will reap what you will sow. Meaning that our actions have consequences.

This whole Universe is based on the law of cause & effect, that is to every event happening, we can attribute one or several causes to it. Then, the effect of suffering must also have its causes- this is logical. And we have to know the root causes of our underlying sufferings. Unfortunately, science does not often go deep to find the origins of suffering & has developed the habit of curing symptoms. From a karmic point of view, the more the suffering, the heavier the karma in terms of negative aspects. This is because karma can be both positive & negative. That is, good actions will lead to good results & bad actions will lead to bad reactions. The sufferings of our next birth are already determined at the time of our death since we have already accumulated all the necessary karma of that life. There is no way that the accumulated actions can be erased at the time of death, except by leading a spiritual life. The karma of a spiritual aspirant can be nullified by the Grace of God- we must make ourselves deserving of this.

This is why spirituality puts emphasis on behaviour. Proper behaviour is mandatory for the betterment of the human race as well as of society. But modernism & material life have completely shrouded this important aspect of our life due to the phenomenon of liberty & freedom. The degree of suffering is verily more dependent on the nature of our behaviour rather than on the practice of religious rituals & festivals. There is in fact a direct relationship between the nature of our behaviour & the suffering of this life as well as of future lives.

This world has a dual nature, meaning that everything which exists has its opposite just like: light & darkness, love & hate. Human nature is quite fragile & is subject to the influence of energies. Good energies uplift us whereas low & dense energies affect us adversely. When we are subject to regular negative energies generated either by ourselves or sent by other people to us, then we are also bound to suffer. For example, if we are pessimistic by nature, then we shall inevitably paint a dull picture of our own lives as we see everything as black & evil. So, this attitude will definitely make us suffer & without knowing that we are the ones creating our miseries!

Again, we see here how knowledge can go a very long way to release us from self made obstacles, prisons & chains. And what is sad is that we can stay in that state for a whole lifetime, without obtaining the proper solution. I would like to mention that the most negative & hurtful energy is the energy of guilt. When we feel guilty either genuinely & even falsely, then the degree to which it affects us is monumental. Many people like to go over the sorrows of the past & to repeatedly regret their course of action or contribution towards the event. This is a great cause of suffering whereby we are chained to the past & we keep the wounds alive by using our memory. Such a mind is indeed our worst enemy & regretfully, some people will find their lives so unbearable that they can commit suicide in such circumstances. Negative thinking will cause us a lot of physical, emotional & mental troubles.

The human body is like a telecommunication antenna, sending out & receiving energies regularly. But, most of us are unconscious of this aspect of our life & we believe we are made of flesh & bones only. We have all seven bodies & more than a hundred energy centres called chakras inside our body. The spirit is one among the seven bodies & is a replica of our shape, except that it is made up solely of energy or electromagnetic vibrations. When we are attending a party, our mood & energy is high due to the pleasant atmosphere of decorations & music. So, we feel positively energised just like after a session of Reiki healing. But, how do we feel when we attend a funeral? Therefore, our body does interact a lot with energy. It is possible to absorb or reject these energies. When a person hates us a lot or is angry at us madly, then that person is sending a huge amount of energy on us. And, if at that moment, our energy is weak, we shall unfortunately absorb a lot of negative energies which will affect us. Other strong negative energies include jealousy, evil eye, lust & anxiety. Our aura, which is an electromagnetic shield of protection all around our body, can protect us from harmful energies. But many people do not even know about the existence of an aura- again an ignorance or lack of knowledge.

Our aura is very sensitive to both positive energy & negative energy. When absorbing too much negative energy, our aura becomes weak & loses its ability to fight strong negative energies.

It may even break & allow harmful energies to get in touch with our physical body & cause illnesses. But our body can also absorb positive energy from another person whose energy is very high, like that of a saint or from a prayer session which has sufficiently raised the energy of the ambient atmosphere. Reiki

initiation is a great way of strengthening our aura & we can immediately feel it. A healing session by an experienced Reiki Master will also heal the broken parts of the aura.

Tense relationships are another incredible source of suffering. Human beings are essentially driven by emotions. We feel great when we are loved & cared for. Our heart chakra, which is the centre of feelings & emotions, is not understood properly. First of all, we do not make the distinction between love & attachment. Both are very powerful emotions & most people like to get attached rather than being loved.

Attachment is a major cause of suffering as it is comparable to slavery- meaning we do not feel well when the master is not present. Attachment makes us dependent on someone else & we feel lost without them! This is not love but loss of freedom & love is freedom itself! And when there is a separation, we do not know how to behave as we are dependent on somebody else for our wellbeing & happiness. True love does not bind two persons together whereas a wedding is exactly this process. Loving is only about sharing sincerely. The famous & most wrongly utilised sentence is surely "**I love you**." It can have so many meanings except the real I love you. Some say I love you to be able to date & hang around, some say it to get in bed together & others say it as they appreciate the physical beauty. Veritably, we do not need to say "**I love you**." We should be able to feel it. So, instead of thinking whether you love someone or if someone loves you, better notice carefully how you feel. Feelings cannot be wrong whereas thoughts can be.

Relationships between parents & children can also be troublesome- this leads to children becoming stressed at an early age. The consequences can be multiple with impacts on health, education & sociability. Some parents are very authoritative as well as ignorant of the proper upbringing of young children & they cause a lot of emotional & mental disturbances to their children. And it is very difficult to help in such situations as the parental ego shall be a major obstacle to counselling & understanding. The children are also powerless to take initiatives as they simply do not know how to get out of such a complex situation. We should be aware that the sufferings of early childhood have a major impact on our behaviour in adult life. I have met many people suffering from diseases which seem to have no medical solution except Reiki healing. I recall one case where a young man lost his mother who was suffering from cancer. He was left with his very authoritative father who could not understand why his son had to follow a psychiatric treatment. After a few sessions, I decided to tell him the truth- he burst into tears. And I told him the only medicine that will work for his son is his love for him. You can imagine how complicated life can be if we do not have the right knowledge & information.

Overthinking is another aspect of our human life that leads to incredible mental suffering. In today's world, the daily stress coupled with the pressures of the modern world has a lot of negative impacts on our mind. And the mind which is not properly trained to fight against the modern world will surely become weak at some point in time. When we get stuck in the rat race to become wealthier, more beautiful & handsome, more educated & more successful professionally, then we are bound to suffer emotionally & mentally if all the set objectives are not met. Frustration is a common ailment today. It is verily the start of many other wellbeing issues. We are faced with so many opportunities today that we cannot seem to make the right decisions. Thus, we keep thinking without reaching a decision, just like the little hamster running on a static spinning wheel in a pet shop! Self-control is a must in this rapidly changing world as well as the power to be satisfied with one's life. If one is able to achieve these two skills, then one shall be less troubled.

The inability to forgive those who have hurt us will also lead to great suffering. Forgiveness is a spiritual dimension which few people know about. And on top of that, even when we are conversant with the benefits of forgiving, we are very reluctant to put it into practice.

Forgiving is a divine tool that helps us to remove anger & frustration from our hearts. It also serves to keep us away from the spiteful actions of our detractors. It is said that: *"to err is human, to forgive is divine."* Thus, we learn from this saying that to make mistakes is human nature, whereas to forgive the mistakes of humans is a divine nature. Then, it is only a question of choice: do we want to live as a human or as a divine being?

> **66**
> *The desire to hurt the culprit or to remain in a state of suffering is stronger than the desire to forgive & forget.*
> **99**

Chapter 5

Meditation & Yoga

> *When the third eye is open, understanding & feeling merge together to create intuition.*

The term yoga is a Sanskrit (ancient Hindu language) word that means the union of the individual self with the Higher Self. This is very often confused with yoga postures. They are not the same. Meditation is a form of yoga as well as recitation of mantras & the act of living as a hermit in renunciation is also called yoga. As such, any religious or spiritual activity which can bring us into a state of union with the Higher Self is called yoga. Because getting into union with God means going back Home, to our source & origin- to become the

> *The act of reunification of the individual with God is the prime objective of a human life.*

real us. Therefore, what we are today is not our real "**us**". But we falsely believe that we are this body & that our relatives, friends, pets, and plants are all different from us. It is only the body which is different. On the inside, we are all one & the same. Our physical eyes do not allow us to feel & see the inner being inside of us whereas when the third eye is open, then we are able to see the divine who lives inside of us.

Meditation is the action of going inside of us to witness the inner world, with our eyes closed. In the physical outer world, we see with our physical eyes. To get access to the inner world which is the controller of the outside world, we have to close our eyes & let the vision appear on our forehead. There is only a small percentage of people in the world who have started the practice of meditation- this is because of the mystery which surrounds the word itself & the type of people generally associated with meditation. When we tell someone that we meditate, immediately there is a strange reaction stipulating that we are not normal beings! The reason is that it is very rare & that the "**common**" man does not indulge in such a practice. On top of that, the material world is in direct opposition to the world of spiritual aspirants who meditate.

Meditators are seen as the odd people of society with whom we should not mingle as they are weird & different from the rest of the population. They are considered as people with whom it will be difficult to adapt & to have a normal conversation. This is a stereotype which is still persisting today, because the strength of the material world in which most people are unknowingly caught up, is excessively high. It will require a great deal of mental power & perseverance to walk on the spiritual path. When I started meditating, after some years, I felt that I no longer wanted to eat meat, fish & eggs. So, I informed my mother about it & she was shocked. She was adamant it was a wrong decision but I maintained my decision as deep down, I was sure this was what I had to do. Meditating regularly will inevitably work on the inner transformation of the person & the inner changes will also definitely be reflected in the outer world of the person in terms of behaviour, lifestyle & attitudes.

Meditation is a fire which can burn all the negativities inside of our body. By negativities, I mean all our attributes which act as hidden veils over our real identity. The veils are numerous & require also a high level of determination to overcome, as resistance to change is huge. Some common examples of these veils include fear, worry, lack of openness, sadness, agitation, anger, etc. All these negative attributes are unfortunately believed to be our "**normal**" way of being as we are unaware of things better than this or unaware that we can lead a better life. Also, since the majority of people around us & with whom we are acquainted are also behaving in the same way, then we erroneously conclude that we are all doing fine! The whole world is behaving in the same way, adopting the same trends & fashions- but does this necessarily mean that this is the best way of life or do we do it as mere followers without questioning? To progress in life, it is very important to ask the right questions- this is called inquisitiveness & is indeed a great quality of a spiritual aspirant. That hunger to know more is the driving force. The more we meditate, the more we get access to superior knowledge. This happens either by exposure to more formal knowledge superbly arranged by divine intervention via books, lectures or the internet or by a phenomenon which is called auric absorption of knowledge. In very deep meditation, we get access to superior knowledge as decided by our Higher Self simply by direct injection into our brain. This happens only in the advanced stages of meditation, whereby God uses his true disciples to convey His messages to the world or to carry out the missions upon which He has decided. All original sacred books have been written by auric transmission & passed on to generations.

When we meditate regularly, we are keeping the spiritual connection on. This is a magnificent advantage over those who do not meditate. As such, our life is better guided & we shall rarely make mistakes. After several years of meditation, a stage arrives where we get answers to all the questions we ask. This is a really beautiful stage as it allows the practitioner to get rid of all confusions that exist in the mind as well as to increase his knowledge. Answers are given in different modes & the serious spiritual student must believe & get used to this way of getting answers. As we cultivate the process of questioning & interpreting the answer codes, then we are sure to make gigantic progress in the spiritual field. Answers can be direct & we clearly hear a voice; they can be in the form of dreams which have to be interpreted, they can be in the form of repeated signs like double numbers and triple numbers, they can be seeing feathers regularly on your way, they can be some types of animals regularly showing up, they can be words spoken by a friend or relative, they can be an article we read somewhere & which has the just the words we need, they can be found in a movie, they can be coins that keep falling from your purse, etc. Factually, the communication mode is numerous & varied but care must be exercised not to miss the answers or to wrongly interpret them. The clue here is to be receptive to the divine world. Without proper receptivity, we shall not be able to crack the codes & progress. How do we become receptive? It is simply by believing firmly in spiritual support, remaining calm & being attentive to our surroundings. In a way, we have to play our part & the divine world will respond lovingly & positively to our actions.

Yoga postures or yoga asana (Hindu term) are postures which we adopt with our body to improve or strengthen our health. There are eighty-four postures which can be categorised into sitting, standing & lying postures. The best time to perform yoga postures is early morning before sunrise and, if possible, to perform in the open for best results. I remember my maternal grandmother who would come regularly to spend school holidays with us telling me so many times: "*You should wake up before sunrise!*" I was a teenager at that time & of course, I could not achieve that feat until I started meditating. The vibration which exists two hours before sunrise is immensely auspicious & is called in Hinduism "**Brahma Muhurta**" or the sacred Brahma duration. Lord Brahma is the God of creation of this whole Universe. Some postures are relatively easy to practice and fall in the beginner category and with daily practice, we can move to postures which are intermediate in difficulty. The advanced postures are complex to practice & will require assistance from an expert in the matter.

Practicing yoga postures is a marvellous way to vitalise all three aspects of body, mind & soul. Some people find it difficult to practice alone & they need to join a weekly class. A monthly class will not be beneficial as the gap between sessions shall be too long. The best practice is daily, to fully benefit from the postures. But the modern human being complains there is not sufficient time every day due to the hectic pace of life. In actual fact, this is dependent on your personal motivation, commitment & goals. I shall also add that our consciousness also plays a vital role in determining the degree of regularity. Many people adopt yoga postures as a routine to relieve themselves from symptoms of illnesses such as hypertension, insomnia, depression, diabetes, moodiness, etc. Others adopt it as a hobby just as a sport activity. It is to be noted here that a competent yoga practitioner is not someone who has mastered all the eighty-four postures! A session of fifteen minutes with a good variation in terms of sitting, standing & lying will do a lot of good to you. As in all cases, practice moderation as an excess of zeal may cause bodily hurts & several weeks of immobility.

Another branch of yoga which must be practiced together with the postures is the breathing exercises called pranayama in Hindu terminology. Breathing exercises endow the body with enhanced energy in a few minutes only. There are simple breathing exercises as well as complex ones which require close supervision by an expert. The primary aim of pranayama is to expand our vital energy, thereby also expanding our consciousness. It is to be noted that breath & consciousness have an intricate relationship. Pranayama also keeps us healthy and cleanses the internal organs & if practiced regularly, will manifest higher knowledge. Spiritual power is closely connected with the practice of pranayama. Like yoga, the best time to practice is early morning on an empty stomach. After doing breathing exercises, it is recommended not to take a shower immediately but to wait for half an hour. After a good session of pranayama, we shall feel energetic, joyful as well as peaceful. Science teaches us that we are breathing in air but this is not the case. Spiritually, we say we are inhaling energy. There are basically ten types of air inside our body & the eleventh one is our spirit itself. Each air has its specific function.

Breathing exercises are basically broken into three parts: inhalation, retention & exhalation. There is a specific ratio between the three parts & it is 1:4:2. This means we must retain our breath four times the duration of our inhalation & then exhale completely in two times the duration of the inhalation. So, you can see it is quite technical but its results enhance the spiritual power. I will state a few of the most common breathing exercises & you can do more research on it. The terminology is in Hindi but explanations are available on the internet; nevertheless, the best way is to approach a competent yoga instructor. So they are: moola bandha, jalandhara bandha, uddiyana bandha, surya bhedana, ujjayi, sitakari, shitali, bhastrika, bhramari, moorchacha & plavini. My favourite pranayama is bhramari as it has given great results in terms of spiritual growth. Now, each technique has its benefits & it is absolutely unnecessary to practice all of them. You need to start with the simple ones & gradually move to the complex ones; but of course, your personal goal & motivation will determine which technique you shall adopt.

The third & last branch of yoga postures is worth mentioning for serious spiritual seekers & it is called salutation to the sun God or "**Surya Namaskar**" in Hindi. It is paying respectful obeisances to the Sun God, who is the sustainer of life in all Universes. Briefly, just for information, there is one Sun in each galaxy of the Universe. Here, in our galaxy called the Milky Way, we have our Sun but there are millions of galaxies in the Universe & therefore millions of Suns. The salutation consists of twelve postures which must be done in a specified sequence. These twelve postures make one complete salutation & twenty-five such salutations are called one round. The practice is done before sunrise, facing East, in the open air & on an empty stomach. This salutation gives great exercise to the body as well as being a great way to pray to the Sun God. It requires quite some stamina to perform one round as it will equal three hundred yoga postures, that is twenty-

five times twelve! If you start to feel uneasy or breathless while performing Surya Namaskar, you should not persist. For serious spiritual seekers, it is extremely important to pray to the Sun God. The salutation can be enhanced by the recitation of different Sun mantras for each of the twelve postures. In this way, the salutation is no more a posture practice but a spiritual practice. And the benefits shall be manifold. I will name the twelve postures in the sequence that they should be performed so that if there is any interest, you can further the research & practice. So, the twelve postures to be practiced in the order written are: Daksha asana, namaskar asana, parvat asana, hastapad asana, ekapadaprasaran asana, Bhudhar asana, ashtangapranipat asana, bhujang asana, Bhudhar asana, ekapadaprasaran asana, hastapad asana, namaskar asana.

Sri Narayana

Chapter 6

Reiki – Natural Healing

Reiki as a tool to increase our energy levels & to heal ourselves is indeed a great opportunity. Simultaneously, there shall be an expansion of the consciousness of the healer because his chakras shall be operating at greater frequencies until one day, the highest possible frequency is reached, if other methods of elevating the soul are practiced. Reiki serves also to cleanse our chakras from harmful self & exterior negativities- thus, our purity increases & we get a good preparation to embark on a spiritual life. Then Reiki can also be used to manifest desires by several techniques- this use of Reiki is more for material goals. At the master level, Reiki meditation is available for the serious student & opens up the spiritual world a bit further. This meditation is based on the direction of specific sounds in each of the seven main chakras from root chakra to crown chakra. It has a great effect on the mental & overall states as all the main chakras are being energised just like the recharging of a flat battery. Another important assistance obtained after the initiation to Reiki is that we have the possibility of clearing many obstacles from past lives. This is a partial cleansing of the karma of the Reiki practitioner. It happens that sufferings in this life, be it mental, emotional & physical are due to the karma of our past lives. This can be attenuated & also completely healed by a master of Reiki. Thus, karma issues can be healed with Reiki. When the karma of an individual gets gradually cleansed, then this automatically is a spiritual growth of high magnitude which may prepare for higher stages of self-development.

The Usui natural way of Reiki healing is based on five principles which are taught at the very first level itself. They are very simple and are described in just one or two lines. However, where the difficulty will surge is in the implementation phase- it is simply not an easy task as you shall see below. It requires a paradigm shift in our attitude & habits but even if we don't practice the five principles, that shall not decrease the effectiveness of the healing sessions or your ability to heal other persons. Here are those five Reiki principles:

- Just for today, I will not be angry.
- Just for today, I will not worry.
- Just for today, I will do my work honestly.
- Just for today, I will be kind to my neighbour & all living things.
- Just for today, I will give thanks for my many blessings.

As you can notice, they are very simple principles & yet endowed with such depth that they gently nudge you to ponder on their meanings & eventual application. All of these principles start with "**just for today**". This sets the appropriate tone for the development of a spiritual life: we only have today, the past is gone & the future has not yet come. A greatly spiritual person lives for his daily routine only & it helps a lot in the management of the process of elevating our soul.

Reiki is a natural healing method which is performed either by laying the palm of the hands on the patient or by transferring the healing energy to the patient without touching. The patient may be present in front of the Reiki healer or found in a different location- both work. The Reiki healing will also be effective even if the person to be treated is located in a different country. This is the power & the beauty of Reiki healing- simple yet very powerful & which can be easily learnt by anyone irrespective of educational status. It may seem impossible to believe in such an occurrence by the common man as the mind is conditioned by the healing practiced by a doctor & cannot conceive of a different method of treatment. I have healed people in Canada, the USA, India, Australia & United Kingdom & I can confirm that this is absolutely normal for Reiki practitioners of level two & onwards.

The origin of Reiki is Tibetan Buddhism; after some time, there was a break in the transmission to other students of Reiki. Then, in the 1800's, it was reintroduced to the world by Dr Mikao Usui, a Japanese doctor. Reiki healing is based on life energy & is a channelled mode of healing, which means that the healer is not using his inner energy. In fact, the Reiki healing has its source in the Universe & all persons who get initiated by a Reiki master become connected with that source. Then, you can use the healing energy at any time you want & in any amount you wish. Reiki healing is not only natural healing but divine healing. There are five levels of Reiki initiation: level 1 for beginners, level 2, level 3 which is a pre-master level, then level 4- the master level & finally level 5 which is the Grand Master level. The capacity to heal increases with the level & is performed by the divine who uses the body of the healer as a channel to transmit the healing energy to the patient.

Since the healing is flowing in the bodies of both the practitioner & the patient, then both get healed! This is one of the most amazing aspects of Reiki. Another superb tool available in the Reiki natural way of healing is the methods used to balance our seven main chakras. Our way of living which includes our thoughts, actions, habits & health directly contributes to the health of our chakras. These can absorb a good deal of negative energies & may even be blocked. A person with several blocked chakras will feel completely demotivated and will be unable to attend to his daily routine. But fortunately, the chakras can be brought back to a normal state by a simple process which lasts four minutes. And the results are immediate!

Reiki is most effective at displacing the accumulation of negative thoughts in our aura- this is a protective electromagnetic field which exists all around our body surface. Non-living materials also have an aura around them due to the vibration of their atoms. At advanced levels of Reiki, a practitioner can indeed see these auras; sometimes, they are of beautiful colours. Our negative thoughts are also electromagnetic & they attach themselves to the aura. If there is an excessive amount of such thoughts, then they shall adversely affect our health. With a cleansing Reiki session, these negative thoughts can be cleared from the system- the overall effect is an immediate feeling of lightness! Many of you have probably read about the dangers of overthinking & negative thoughts- now you have a confirmation of how they affect us. Our aura can be damaged by severe energetic shocks of emotional, mental & physical nature. Once an aura is cracked & open, the physical body is then vulnerable to all energetic & other sorts of threats which affect our wellbeing. A Reiki healing session has the ability to repair a damaged aura. Such an opportunity is indeed a real blessing for those who are keen on looking after their energetic health together with their metabolic health. And the results are fabulous. Such a transformation of low energy to high energy is clearly felt during a session. I have some patients who like to describe how they feel & they always say they have never had such an incredible experience.

In terms of healing diseases, what Reiki does is that it acts on the chakra which is not functioning properly to alleviate the symptoms or to heal it completely. Reiki guarantees that you shall either get relief or enjoy a complete recovery. You don't have to believe in Reiki for it to be effective but you must believe that you are going to get the necessary assistance since it is a divine healing. There is a big difference between believing in yourself & in the divine to get healed and believing in the healer- this must be thoroughly grasped to get enhanced results. Truly, the Reiki healer has no power to drive the session as it is under the control of the divine. Since Reiki helps to get rid of common diseases, then it is effectively preparing the patient for higher levels of awareness if there is an interest. Of course, not all persons have a spiritual search at the back of their minds- some just want to be healed but I would like to point out it is a golden opportunity which gets wasted if we don't probe deeper into the spiritual aspects of Reiki.

A healing session gives the patient a lot of indication as to his personality & character. For instance, the same beautiful auric colours which can be seen in deep meditation can also be seen during a healing session. This is the way Reiki communicates with the patient to inform him of deeper inner aspects of his existence. And it is a tremendous experience for a strictly non spiritual person to see such colours appearing on the forehead. When the colours are decoded, then the patient will have more insight into himself & the nature of his disease. For example, seeing a green colour means a compassionate nature whereas a purple colour means a spiritual nature. Sometimes the patient will have visions which give indications of where other deeper problems may be lying. The visions could be of your childhood, of people you have never met, of Gods & Goddesses, of the sky, of the Universe, of the oceans and many more. Each has its own meaning & will be interpreted by the Reiki healer. The same visions can appear during the initiation process. Over and above the visions, the patient will experience a fantastic feeling of peace, joy & inner beauty. This feeling will not last for long but it does indicate that our inner health, awareness & personal vibration can be altered by divine energy. Unfortunately, in most cases, the patients do not take the time to analyse what has happened to their energy & what they must do to repeat & keep such an experience. It will only happen if there is a wish to pursue further and to try to repeat the experience by yourself. Very few adopt this important decision.

Reiki is not a religion & will not require that you change your beliefs, cultures & traditions. There are no rituals to be performed but only a dedication to practice all the tools that are available at each different level. The initiation to Reiki does not involve any ritual & is made up of standard, universal steps which the Reiki master performs in the name of the person. An initiation is a stunning & unforgettable experience. At that very moment just after the initiation is over, the feelings are quite overwhelming. The Reiki student will have some exercises to practice daily & weekly to keep up the process of transformation. This is where most students fail as they don't have enough willpower to sustain the important shift of internal energy which occurred during the initiation. Because in essence, the role of Reiki is to transform our inner energy for better health & coupled with the increased energy, we can get access to the spiritual world. As is the case with any spiritual practice, regularity & dedication are the keys to success. Unfortunately, the material world will oppose itself strongly against the adoption of a spiritual life.

There is another branch of Reiki which can be mastered by an enthusiastic student- it is the domain of Reiki surgery. As incredible as this may sound, Reiki can be used to perform surgery without cutting open a patient. It is used to remove kidney stones, to unclog arteries, to remove cysts & tumours & many more. And it works very well, but for this, the healer must check whether the surgery will yield the required results. Most of the time it is a successful attempt but when the suffering is a karmic suffering, then the healing will not happen. The advantages of such healing are enormous as there is no anaesthesia, no admission to a hospital, no use of a scalpel to open the body, no bleeding & no pain. There is also no loss of working days! But the sessions are longer, typically two months of treatment & will depend on the nature of the problem- for example, a prostate cancer six centimetres in diameter will take longer time than a one-centimetre cancer. Optimum health is mandatory in the process of spiritual growth, People with bad health can also try, but the willpower of a sick person is usually low due to regular suffering. Exceptions do exist for sick persons who manage to overcome their weaknesses & persevere along the Path of enlightenment. It is all a question of attitude & mental strength.

As you can see, Reiki may play an important role in spiritual development. It only depends on the individual- what he decides to do in his life. Then, everything will flow naturally from this decision. What has happened now with this explanation of Reiki healing is that you are conscious of what exists. Doubts can arise, which is perfectly alright. But it is only the persons who are adventurous & willing to learn new phenomena who will succeed on the spiritual Path. The spiritual qualities involved here are fearlessness & openness: both are required to push ahead on the Path of self-realisation. It is not wrong to stay as a mere human being; but then, we shall never know our true identity. Living in a world of illusion will be very tricky in the sense that we shall miss the opportunities to increase awareness of ourselves. Ignorance will predominate & will certainly trigger its corresponding load of suffering.

Chapter 7

The Divine World

> *The Almighty God created a material world & a divine world. The divine world rules over the physical.*

This Universe is made up of both spiritual planets & material planets. Our Earth is the lowest material planet which exists & this is why suffering is at its peak here. There exist higher material planets in other galaxies, not yet discovered by man, where the quality of life is better than on Earth. And then, there also exist spiritual planets where life is purely spiritual. Science, due to its latest research, is now 99% sure that life exists elsewhere. So, it is coming in line with the already available knowledge in spiritual textbooks. The existence of demigods, angels & ascended Masters form altogether what is called the divine world. In Hinduism, the term demigod is used to differentiate between the Supreme God who is free, has no wife & no children, has no shape, has no beginning & no end & does not take part in material issues. Demigods come into existence either by birth or by actions. In Christianity & Islam, the same demigods exist as in Hinduism, but they have different

names. In an effort to elevate our souls, we have to understand how the Universe operates.

The demigods are assigned the management of the material world & because they have limited powers compared to the Absolute God, then they are bound to make mistakes. As such, they often have to seek higher counselling for the sake of correcting affairs which are not going on well. All demigods have a body which they will have to surrender at appointed divine timings. However, their duration of life cannot be compared to the one hundred years of human life- they live up to billions of years. Now, this may seem to be a very long duration but from the perspective of the Universe, this is only a blink of the eye. Next, a billion years of life duration is not eternity but only immortality. So demi-Gods are also mortals by definition. Only the Absolute God is eternal. Human beings pray to demigods for the accomplishment of material desires such as: to become rich, to get married, to get children, to be employed, etc. But it must be known that the Absolute God is aware of everything. If He does not approve of a human request, then nothing will happen even if the demigod wants to grant the request. To obtain spiritual powers & reach eternity, we have to pray to the one & only Eternal God. This must be clearly understood by the spiritual aspirant.

At the time of creation, God decided that angels would be the way to connect the physical world with the divine world. They are viewed as winged divine beings, both male & female, who are at the disposition of human beings for divine assistance. But they are essentially energetic beings without a body & they can be at different places helping different persons. As such, at birth, all human beings are assigned three guardian angels who are our personal guides. Of this, few people are aware of their existence. Angels are available for any kind of help at any time- we only have to call out to them to get their loving assistance. However, their methods of communication must be well understood to be able to get the message correctly. The messages are most of the time of the indirect type.

A very simple yet effective way by which angels communicate with us is through double, triple & quadruple digits like 11, 333, 8888, 4747, 55, etc. If you encounter such numbers regularly on the clock, on the number plate of cars, on street names, on the battery level of your phone, or on television, then this is a sign that the angels are trying to draw your attention & communicate with you. For some people, it will mean just a coincidence but if you think deeply about it, what is the probability of seeing repeated digits or even the same digits, you will find that it is very small. When I started to see repeated digits,

my first reaction was "*Oh, this is nice!*". Then gradually, the frequency started increasing & I started to realise that something is going on. So, I started to test the issue. And I started to ask a simple question & request an answer. And it happened! Just after a few minutes, I would see a repeated pattern. And when I checked the interpretation online, I was surprised to see I had my answer. Each repeated number will have both general & specific meanings. It is up to you to find out which meaning applies to your situation. I also recall sometimes I did not understand the answers at all. And I said to myself if this is really happening & that I am being heard, I can surely ask for a clearer & more precise answer- and the explanations became clearer! Of course, the conversation must be done with utmost respect & after getting answers, you must say thank you because this is not to be treated as a game. Fooling around with the divine world is certainly not the right attitude although I know some people would be inclined to do so. That is why the concept of being "**chosen**" arises. You must have the proper energy to be able to converse with the divine world. It is available to all, twenty-four hours a day- of this, I am 100% sure. You just have to ensure you get enrolled & to keep your admission secure. If you are still doubtful about this, I can safely inform you that when I posted a video on TikTok on the matter, it reached 68,000 views in a few days & more than 170,000 views in two weeks, with so many acknowledgements from the public of their own experience.

I shall now give a brief meaning of some very interesting repeating digits. 11 means the master number & that you have the potential to rise spiritually. It tells about your connection with the spiritual world. It can also mean you are stressed & that you should calm down. 22 is about teamwork & that you are sensitive to divine energies. You have a lot of ideas and you should express them. 1111 is a fabulous number & you should pay attention to what you were thinking just at that moment you saw the number as it will materialize. If it was a negative feeling, you can just ask to cancel your request. 1155 is about trusting yourself with the decisions you are making. It also means that changes are on the way. 1616 means to stay positive as it is positivity which attracts good people & good things in life. The possibility of repeating numbers is huge & seeing them together with a proper interpretation will serve as a great compass in your life. After this experience, I started using angel cards for predictions and this time, it was so amazing to see the cards pop out of the deck as if an invisible hand was picking them up. And as usual, the answers were right on the dot!

There are also seven main angels, called Archangels, who work directly under the supervision of God & their divine powers are greater than the guardian angels. The most common archangels are Michael, Uriel, Gabriel & Raphael. Once we develop a relationship with them by regularly calling for help, they become a great support for us. Archangel Michael is called the messenger of God & he responds to our requests especially when we need protection of any kind. Archangel Raphael has a special green flame of light which is very helpful to heal ourselves of any kind of disease. Care must be exercised when working with angels to thank them heartily when your wish is granted. They do not like ungrateful people & you might find yourself cut off from their loving help if ungratefulness is continuously practiced. They will never harm you but they can stop responding. Now, it is a very serious matter to start dealing with the divine world believing that you shall behave exactly as you deal with human beings. Respect & attention are vital to succeed in catching their attention to keep the connection ongoing.

In every hour that passes, an angel is assigned for every twenty minutes. This means that in every hour, we have three specific angels available. It is not necessary to know their names- simply asking for help will catch their attention. This is the way the divine world operates. Very often, when you observe the same double-hour clock repeating, then it means that particular angel is your guardian angel. Angels also have specific tasks assigned to them although they all have enough divine power to tackle most of our problems. We have angels for matters of love, relationships, protection, healing, support, destruction, spiritual ascension, etc. Angels are available for any kind of help & you should not hesitate to call on them. Care should be exercised as they know exactly what you are thinking because if you tend to be dishonest, then the communication may be stopped. The divine world expects us to rise to our divine nature & it will be very tolerant in the beginning as this is an unknown world for us. But lessons that have been learnt must not be forgotten & should be applied at all times.

With regards to the Ascended Masters, these are human beings who have been able to reach the perfection of human life & are in communion with the Eternal God. When they are living on Earth, their lives are dedicated to the assistance & the upliftment of the human race. When they die, they may or may not continue to help the human race. They offer their loving help to all those who are deserving even after they have left this Earth. Sometimes, they also choose to come back to continue service or if they are appointed by the Eternal God for specific missions. One of the most ancient Ascended Masters is Mahavatar Babaji & it is said that one gets a blessing only by stating his name. My beloved spiritual master Sri Sri Paramahansa Yogananda is also an Ascended Master & he has a lot of contributions to the spiritual work that I am doing today.

The method of connecting to the divine world is a conversation, aloud or silent- both work. After sending a request, we must patiently wait for the response, which I have mentioned shall be by signs. So, we must also observe what signs we receive because the chances of missing the answers also exist. It is also very important to be open & to drop any kind of expectations to your questions. Some people ask questions & they already wish that the answers be in the way they are expecting- this is not a good approach. The divine answer has to be accepted as it is. And one thing that must be avoided at all costs is to repeat the same questions. Repeating questions will not yield different answers. We must also be willing to accept that not all our problems can be solved by divine intervention. There are problems which are karmic & which we have to go through for a certain duration or for our whole lifetime.

This whole nature exists in duality & therefore everything that exists has its contrary. Thus, the contrary of the divine is evil. Evil is not an original creation by the Absolute God- it is a byproduct of the actions of all created beings due to a deviation from moral & ethical principles. When there is deviation, then evil takes birth- if there are no deviations, then evil does not exist. For example, until people do not consume excess sugar, then diabetes would have never existed! In a land where the population is knowledgeable about the risks of excess dietary sugar, then diabetes does not exist in that country. Evil is a secondary reaction or a subsequent effect. Furthermore, evil actions germinate in the mind & heart which have lost their purity & are influenced greatly by material gains to satisfy bodily pleasures & wishes. That is how evil is generated. A pure mind & heart shall never cause harm- this is logical. Evil nature is not granted communication with the divine world. This is logical as the energies are not compatible. The same thing happens on Earth in terms of incompatibility. People are born under three categories of nature: human, divine & evil. When we associate with people of evil nature, then we suffer a lot.

There are three great evils on Earth which the weak & conditioned mind cannot control: greed, anger & lust. All evil actions can be categorized under those three evils. Corruption, obesity & theft fall under greed. Crimes, disagreements & verbal/physical abuse fall under anger. Extra-marital affairs, cheating, rape & other sexual abuse fall under lust. How do all these evils arise? Simply by deviations from our true nature, our divine nature. This is called falling & is the reason why we take birth on Earth. And after a great deal of accumulation of sins & offenses when we are on higher planets, then we literally fall from these spiritual & higher material planets to obtain a life of miseries on Earth. But the illusion is that we believe that this place is a magnificent one to live in, due to the captivating & irresistible wonders of the sumptuous material world. As you evolve spiritually, you will find that you will even start to feel fed up with your body!

Buddhism teaches its devotees to develop a sense of rejection of their bodies in order to climb higher spiritually. But I prefer that it happens naturally at its appointed time- we cannot force spiritual growth or the elevation of our soul.

Chapter 8

Spirituality v/s Religion & Universal Knowledge

> *You can live to the highest of your potential if you believe in yourself & trust that you are not a simple mortal being.*

Formal knowledge is learning by the means which society has put at our disposal. In developed countries, we get access to education by a system which has been developed several centuries ago & on which our society depends. It is a gradual form of learning which exposes the student to appropriate education based on age. This type of learning is more of a preparation to meet the standards which society has set, that is to get a job, earn a living & be self-sufficient. The more education you have, the greater your salary. This is the message that is sent out to all the students, as if without formal education, we are a rejection of society. But it happens that even a few who do not have high education, still manage to do even better in terms of revenue than those who are well-educated! This is life. So, the system is imposed on us & we all follow it without questioning & by fear of being an outlaw or rejected by our relatives & friends. Society places a great deal of importance on educational success & once in a while, we do see a drama whereby students commit suicide due to poor results. And then, as far as possible, society tries to accommodate those who cannot complete their education fully by other arrangements; or if not, these students are left on their own.

The subjects of education are indeed varied & huge in diversity. We study for about twenty to twenty-two years of our life if we manage to go up to the university level. Then, for the remaining years, we rarely take on classes & now, we go on with working or founding a family. So, we are asked to live & nobody teaches us what life is about. That is a huge flaw of our society. We are never equipped with the right knowledge about ourselves, life & the Universe in order to live a good life. An exception exists here for those who take up psychology, medical & healing courses & who at least, acquire knowledge about the human body & about the behaviour of human beings. But there is much more knowledge than that. And this is the domain of Universal Knowledge. In a previous chapter, I mentioned it is science, politicians & business leaders who are driving the world. And they are certainly not knowledgeable about religious & spiritual matters, which are essential pillars of society.

And it becomes more dramatic when we know that most people belong to a certain religion except for the atheists. This happens because religion also is unable to teach its followers the basics of spiritual knowledge, which is so important for a balanced life. Religious rituals & festivals only give a religious identity, creating differences in terms of "**we**" & "**they**". Some even go to the point of stating that they are superior to others. All this leads unfortunately to racism, fanaticism & also extremism. The result is? We are all divided & only co-living with each other.

The big family of the human race as children of God is absent. Religion also operates at the level of demigods; this is very important to understand. Although most of the great religions do have knowledge of the Eternal God, they simply do not adventure themselves in sharing this knowledge.

The reason, I believe, is that the followers are not ready to adopt a stricter & disciplined way of life. Let me give a clear example to substantiate this. In most religions, when celebrating festivals, the devotees know that they have to fast for several days ranging from three to forty days. What is fasting? Generally, it consists of the absence of non-vegetarian foods, sleeping on the ground, no sex, no alcoholic drinks & cigarettes, and control of negative thoughts (rarely done, but I state it nonetheless). Why is this done? To please the God we are praying & mostly to follow the festival procedures. But what happens after the festival? We go back to the usual "**forbidden routine**" until the next festival comes. The point I want to make here is we alternate from good procedures to bad procedures during our whole lifetime! Then, how are we supposed to grow & learn in the religious environment? Some learning will happen but it shall be limited. We have to open up & look for more. And most of all, good procedures of life must not be sporadic but a daily routine. But, most of us feel satisfied with the religious belonging & believe wrongly that this is "**it**" & that there is nothing greater beyond. Most probably since the requirements of being religious are fairly easy to handle & will not necessitate a colossal amount of patience & self-discipline, this eventually leads to a greater number of followers.

The human being is essentially a centre of feelings or more exactly, this is the most common trend which is adopted. It is as if we have not learnt to behave in any other way other than choosing the emotional path. Women are more emotional than men- this is a fact. Men tend to use logic more often than emotions. Why are emotions driving our lives? It is simply because emotions trigger our senses a lot & due to the fact that most of us are attached to our senses; we like to feel & to live through our senses. Marketing & social media specialists will agree here that extensive use of emotions is made for advertising products & services as well as for internet videos to go viral. If the emotional factor is not present, then it is highly likely that the advertising program/or internet video will not meet the expected objectives. And what to say about people who are in love? Everything they do together or separately generates loads of emotions!

Similarly, religion is more popular than spirituality as it generates more emotions. When you spot many people gathered well dressed, smell the perfume of incense sticks, see the statues richly decorated, hear the prayers being recited or sung with music, eat food together with all devotees, etc, then many of your senses are triggered- you feel good. On the other hand, spirituality teaches us to have control over our emotions! You can observe the major difference. That is why the spiritual Path has fewer followers. A spiritual life requires hard work or penance, strict discipline & unwavering faith. Religion at the level of temples, churches, mosques, etc is practiced in great fervour during festivals only whereas spirituality is a daily practice- there are no celebrations to be enjoyed except for Guru Purnima (full moon dedicated to all Gurus in Hinduism). Definitely, a spiritual approach has more difficulties compared to a religious approach, but that does not mean we should refrain from doing it. Yet, the fruits of spiritual practice are very rewarding.

Spirituality is a domain whereby the mind is the central pillar of the practices- we meditate with the power of the mind, we develop self-control to gain mastery over the fickle mind, we use the mind to control our emotions & sensuality & finally, we cleanse the mind from negativities & impurities. Then, we also make use of the breath like in breathing exercises of yoga to increase the thickness of our aura & achieve higher levels of consciousness.

Last, we use our internal energy to reach a state of peace & calm so that our external world also is peaceful & calm. Religion makes use of pictures & statues of several deities for prayers & worship, whereas in spirituality, we are taught that there is only one God who has no shape or body, who can take any shape or body, who was not born, who will not die, who has no wife & no children, who has no beginning & no end, who is present in both living & non-living things & who is the origin of all creations. In Hinduism, this matter has been thoroughly debated & it is said affirmed that praying

to the formless God is called the "**Nirguna**" prayer whereas praying to deities who have a form is called the "**Saguna**" prayer. You are now aware that this Universal Knowledge exists & when you get access to it, there is one last step to be performed, that is to believe it's the truth & to implement it in your lives.

Enlightened Masters teach us that the Path or Way to reach the spiritual world is through the rectification of the mind. All major religions believe & accept that there is a Higher Mind, a Cosmic Mind or a Holy Spirit. It might take several births for a person to reach the maximum potential by the practice of religion & it might as well also never happen. But with spirituality, we can perfect our soul in this birth itself because such is its power. And if you are blessed to have a genuine Guru in your life, then you are guaranteed to reach the highest spiritual state, provided you behave as a proper student. That is also very important. The mental disposition of the student is crucial in spiritual matters & it is something which has no great impact on religion. We can skip a festival, a fasting, a ritual, be absent in a prayer session or mass and not concentrate on the prayer session, it will have little or no impact on our development. But this is not the case for spiritual matters- integrity, seriousness, discipline are extremely important. And the spiritual master will know among the students who are the ones who are best suited for higher knowledge.

Over & above religious & spiritual knowledge, there also exists a bank of Universal Knowledge. Everything I am writing in this book comes from this bank, which is available to all who genuinely want to walk on the spiritual Path & find the Way. Universal Knowledge is as vast as the Universe itself. The more you progress, the more you get access to higher knowledge. Ascended Masters of any era take valuable knowledge from this source to share with the world at appointed divine timings. But you must realise that everything happens by the will of God. During his time on Earth, Lord Buddha informed that all that He is sharing does not come from Him but from the bank of Universal Knowledge.

This is the process- the more you elevate your soul, the more this source opens up to you. It requires a great deal of sustained efforts to come to this level but divine help is always available to all earnest seekers of the Truth. Knowledge of the material plane of life is small compared to Universal Knowledge- however, a great deal of material knowledge is helping the human race to sort out some of its difficulties. Other knowledge is only for pleasurable activities or educative purposes. The impact & importance of Universal Knowledge are comparable to the effects of a revolution- it is the closing of the chapters of an old life & the start of a completely new life. It is letting go of past behaviours, things & people who are no more serving us anymore. The term "**rebirth**" is worth mentioning here as there is abundant literature on this today- this is what exactly happens after sufficient exposure to & practice of Universal Knowledge.

Higher Knowledge promises a great liberation to the sincere & earnest seeker. Freedom! If you think about it, how many people are free today? If you are employed, you spend 80% of the week working. If you are married, the remaining 20% is to look after the family during the week as well as during the weekend. Then, where is time left for "**you**"? But these are the norms of society. We follow, barely asking questions if we can choose another path & we are caught in the invisible material net. Of course, we

> *Liberation is at the centre of all spiritual practices & is exactly a point of convergence of all of these practices. This is what all seekers of the Truth look for- that liberation from all earthly bondages.*

need some Harmony inmaterial revenue to live but it can be a strict minimum. Even without material comforts & money, life can be sustained- you only have to surrender to the Almighty God. The thing is we have not been used or exposed to such realities & in our conditioned state, we have a cornered & limited vision of the dimensions of the Truth. If you can recall how Lord Krishna fed the whole world with just one grain of cooked rice to protect one of His great devotes or how Lord Jesus fed numerous people with just some bread & fish, then where is your faith?

In fact, it is recommended to save enough money to sustain a spiritual life, which can start at around forty years of age. With the savings, you can live a simple life alone. This is what is recommended in the Hindu holy scriptures- that after twenty to twenty-five years of married life, you should adopt the renounced way of life to find the Truth. But very few of us will dare to follow this procedure & yet all of us are craving for peace, health, satisfaction & stable relationships. Can the material world grant us all of these simultaneously in this life? Can a spiritual life bless you with such divine gifts? The answer is yes. Because all these qualities you are looking for are to be obtained as divine gifts from the divine world. And we need to deserve them to get them- no corruption & no bypassing are possible.

Chapter 9

The Ego: What You Should Know

The human being is made of up a soul, mind, intelligence, ego & body. All these attributes form our nature & the highest performer is the soul & the lowest is the body. We can act through all of these five attributes. Our actions are great & full of divine power when we act with our soul- this is a rare event. Most people act with the remaining four attributes, with the majority acting with the ego & body. The common man associates ego with pride, haughtiness & sarcasm. While this may true, it is only a partial definition of ego. A short & brief definition of ego is intelligence which has been falsified & contaminated by impurities. I like this definition as it shows the importance of purity in human life & the dangers of impurity.

The understanding of the functions of the ego is vital for serious spiritual aspirants as it plays a great part in the process of elevating the soul or enlightenment. Ego acts in such a way that it makes us deviate from our divine nature. Great psychologists have studied the ego & one of them, Carl Jung, has found that the ego is found mostly in adults and not in children. And he made a fantastic finding related to self-realisation & stated for us to find our true selves, we should develop childlike consciousness! And who is a child? It is purity & innocence. The ego is the exact contrary of purity & innocence. To reach a high state of consciousness, we must let this child's consciousness be born again out of our adult nature. This is indeed a huge task at hand as it implies a great transformation, which most of us are not willing to adopt. And Lord Jesus does state this in the Bible. Now, there is a big difference between childlike nature & childish nature. The latter is more of immature & irresponsible traits whereas the former is the development of innocence & purity. Innocence means compassion coupled with openness. Purity relates to aversion to fault-finding & retaliation. Openness is the ability to learn, to be curious, to have trust, and to stop thinking of the future. That is how a child functions. And do you identify what adults do with their lives?

Another way to see how ego is present is to have a look at the degree of reactions in our daily lives. The act of reacting is food to the ego, as the latter requires nourishment to be alive & active. So, what is reacting? It is our emotional, physical & mental triggers to what changes our energy, be it positively or negatively. When there is a reaction by one or more external or internal stimuli, the ego is in action. As an example, you are in a dense traffic jam while going to the office. And your immediate possible responses are irritability, harsh language, shouting, restlessness, etc. This is full use of ego. On the contrary, the other alternative, which you rarely think about, is to remain calm & undisturbed by saying to yourself: "*I don't have any control over this traffic jam, so let me stay calm.*" You will notice how it is a pure question of mindset to decide intentionally if you are going to affect your energy or not. This is an example based on negative emotions; it works the same way for positive emotions. Suppose your favourite football team wins the league title & you are in the stadium. You will shout, jump with joy, sing, cry, bang on posters, etc. You will also celebrate after the match with your friends. Although it is a positive energy which has been generated, your state of energy has been altered & it is still nourishment to our enemy, the ego.

Our energy should not be disturbed by any outside or inside events. Internal triggers are mostly diseases which affect our wellbeing & our morale. Both of these will create an imbalance & subsequent reaction. It is not an easy task to get control over the ego. But, with proper training & perseverance, even the hardest of all tasks is possible. The first step is to become conscious of how the ego functions- this is Universal Knowledge. Then the application of the solution is required. Of course, there shall be immense resistance to this inner transformation but every time you fail, you have to start over again. A word of caution here is very important with respect to the proper "**treatment**" of ego. It is not the suppression of the ego that is demanded but its transcending. As the more you suppress it, the greater shall be the resistance. Transcending is equal to overcoming, going above or gaining mastery over something which blocks us.

You certainly don't have to worry about how this ego management should be performed in terms of whether you will have enough opportunities to practice. I can guarantee you that life will provide you with more than enough opportunities to practice transcending ego because this is the way life is! You only need to be conscious each time & just stay calm. What I have just explained is a great spiritual lesson & forms part of the process of elevating your soul. It is the soul which must be happy, not the mind, not the body & not the heart! And this knowledge is not from me but from the pool of Universal Knowledge in which all Masters dive to transform. The key element here is to stay calm in whatever situation life is putting you into. It seems hard & impossible when exposed to such an idea, but trust me, it works. The trick here is to be able to carefully & mindfully sense that you are being submerged by your emotions. At this point, you should not give a name to what you are feeling- just observe & that is how you weaken the ego & strengthen your mind. We have been trained to react rather than respond- all the seven billion people on Earth less the Masters live their lives this way. But change is the name of the game, isn't it? That is what is taught in management classes, lectures & conferences. Well, it is the same application in life. Change is dynamism, laziness or complacency is a slow death. Change is small in intensity, transformation is greater & still more, and a revolution is greatest. To walk & reach the unknown, it is a revolution which is required.

Meditation is a great way to tackle the transcending of the ego. You will recall that I said meditation is a transformative fire which has the capability to burn down the negativities inside your body. The ego is also one such negativity. Regular practice will help the serious spiritual aspirant to progress to higher states of consciousness, which is attainable by overcoming the ego. The act of meditation helps in achieving greater states of calmness & interior peace. The calmer & more peaceful a person is, the lesser the amount of ego in that person. But meditation alone will not complete the job- a conscious & methodical application of the overcoming of the ego must be performed. This is because in the preliminary stages of meditation, the state of calmness & peace disappears after some duration, which varies from individual to individual. For some, it is a few minutes; and for others, it can be several hours. Still, for others, they don't even reach that state of calmness & peace. When we meditate, we shall make progress, that's for sure. But there is a danger here- it is that the whole system for the person is getting elevated; that is to say: the soul, the mind, the intelligence & the ego as well! The body does not get elevated as it is physical.

I have seen students who after several years of mediation, were becoming prouder and more arrogant due to the very fact that the ego has not been overcome. Sadly, some spiritual masters also have this ego in their system and their students are not able to detect this. A knowledgeable & responsible master will lead the students properly & not haphazardly. Religion does not tackle the problems of the ego- it is only centred on the practice of rituals which have absolutely no effect on the transcending of the ego. In Hinduism, people seem to have forgotten that Shri Narayan (The Primal Spirit) said in the Shrimad Bhagavatam 3:31.16 & Bhagavad Gita 18:66: *"Forget all rites & rituals, just surrender unto Me."* What is surrender? It is an act of humility to submit oneself to the Almighty God or to a spiritual master. And what is humility? It is the absence of ego. You see how beautifully every higher knowledge is interconnected to each other. But we must take time to study & meditate on the power of knowledge.

In Christianity, it is mentioned to devotees that they must become like children, who are the symbol of innocence & purity. Do innocent & pure beings possess egos? Absolutely not! Now you have the proof that the knowledge is available in most religions- it will suffice that the management committees of temples & churches do their job correctly. And that they start to disseminate this knowledge regularly during prayer gatherings & masses. Then, the population will know because, without proper guidance, the population is lost. In Hinduism, this is exactly the job of a Guru (spiritual master). **"Gu"** means darkness and **"ru"** means removal. In Christianity,

Lord Jesus does talk about the shepherd (Guru) who will lead the sheep (population). A few weeks ago, I heard Christians sing a prayer on the shepherd during the funeral mass of my friend's deceased mother. I was so happy to hear that prayer, with a musical arrangement from two guitars.

The act of criticising & analysing is unfortunately also a great way to nourish the ego. Very few people are aware of this. And it seems today that lots of people have become experts in the art of analysing & criticising! If sometimes, you could record & listen to speeches during arguments & heated debates, indeed you would be very surprised & probably feeling ashamed. This is the ego in its most popular form- critics are everywhere: on people's lips, on radio & on social media. I will state here that social media is a fantastic way of increasing the ego of a person, due to the freedom of expression via comments. The inward God who resides in our heart is a silent observer. That is exactly how we should behave for the purpose of promoting our divine nature- we should observe only & rarely criticise. You will find that this is very hard to implement because every time your ego will prompt you to defend either your self-image or self-identity or self-esteem.

This defence mechanism of the ego is an involuntary action that is performed by all of us without us even noticing that it is at work! And try to tell a person that he or she possesses ego. Immediately a verbal clash will ensue. The ego uses defence as it knows that deep inside you are fearful & protective of yourself, more precisely the self which is not the real you. And this is the beauty of Universal Knowledge- it teaches us the difference between the real "**us**" & the false "**us**." If we are fully aware of our divine identity & we live by this very identity every day, then how can we be protective of our self-image, self-identity & self-esteem? We shall not even pay attention to them as they are not real. This is the power of spirituality & how knowledge burns down all ignorance to make us transform into our real nature. That is why it is said that everything around us is unreal & that we have to look for Reality- it is because the ego has falsified everything. Gradually as the ego is weakened, it loses its grip over the control of our emotions & one day arrives when emotions no longer affect us.

With this knowledge, you will now understand yourself & the world around you. Both are important. Knowing oneself is called intelligence, whereas knowing others is wisdom. To substantiate the lessons of this chapter, I would like to quote from the Bhagavad Gita 6:8 where Lord Krishna gives this beautiful knowledge to Arjuna:" *Humility, pridelessness, non-violence, tolerance, simplicity, approaching a bona fide spiritual master, cleanliness, steadiness, self-control, renunciation of the objects of sense gratification, absence of ego, the perception of the evil of birth, death, old age & disease, detachment, freedom from entanglement with children, wife,*  *home & the rest, even-mindedness amid pleasant & unpleasant events, constant & unalloyed devotion to Me, aspiring to live a solitary life, detachment from the general mass of people, accepting the importance of self-realisation & philosophical search for the Absolute Truth- all these I declare to be knowledge, and besides this, whatever there may be is ignorance."* Just ponder on how direct & clear the message is.

Chapter 10

The Nine Types of Prayers to God

> *To meditate eyes closed or to write in a journal is*
> *the same task- you are connecting with your mind.*
> *(Chinese Proverb)*

One of the simplest ways to elevate our soul & get closer to God is by praying. Prayer is the action of showing devotion to our Creator. Indeed, when properly practiced, prayer is very powerful. We often hear about the issue of prayers being unanswered & how to go about this. Human beings are constantly making demands to obtain material satisfaction in their personal lives- it is as if their wants are unlimited! The degree of dissatisfaction remains at a fairly high level & the frustrated  human being then lives a miserable life. There are two aspects here that need to be understood. On one hand, we have human beings treating God as a wish-giver & on the other hand, we have the incessant flow of desires, characteristic of the modern, material world. The wish-giving God is thus like the parents who fulfill the desires of His children. And the relentless desires are the fallible nature of the human race. To refrain from desires is to open up to our divine nature.

Behind 99% of worldwide prayers, wishes are operating behind the curtains. Doesn't God know what is in our minds even if we don't ask? What would happen if we stopped asking & lived a life of plain simplicity & satisfaction? The best of all prayers is the cultivation of love for God. The more you love God, the more your desires shall be fulfilled, even the unstated ones. Because God knows what to give you. Trust is the barrier that comes in between us and the God we pray. So, the preliminary ingredients of an effective prayer are love for God and trust in God. Then, it is crucial to have a strong intention of praying- that is we must be determined & serious about our prayer. It should not be a mechanical prayer just for the sake of doing it or just to follow either parental instructions or traditions & culture. When I was a teenager, I used to pray just because it is the tradition in Hindu families to light a lamp in the morning & evening. I was not doing it with real purpose & intention but the power of prayers is totally different when the intention is set. Because the God inside our hearts knows very well about our honesty & integrity. These two qualities are also vital in spiritual progress.

Concentration is another fundamental aspect for a prayer to be effective. Intention & seriousness will already set the tone for a good session of prayer. Concentration will increase it even further because now there is focus. I always inform my followers that prayer is also most effective when performed alone for the simple reason that concentration is greatest in loneliness & not in a crowd of hundreds & thousands of devotees. When we are distracted by a crowd, how can there be concentration? But even in solitude praying, there may very well be internal disturbances caused by the thoughts which we cannot control. It is customary that for the person who has not yet developed mastery over the mind, that as soon as the eyes are closed, thoughts start to flood the mind. And we are so helpless in trying to stop the incessant flow of thoughts. At this stage, it is worth noting that it is either the subconscious mind or the imagination which is dominating. How can there again be concentration on God in such circumstances? It is important to realise how important it is to have a careful preparation for an effective prayer session. So, if prayers are not performed correctly, then how can we expect manifestation? The level of our personal vibration is also important to effectively implement all the characteristics of a good prayer, which are: concentration, honesty, integrity, intention & control of thoughts. All these are states of our internal energy.

The first type of prayer consists of hearing ritualistic prayers performed at home or in a religious place. When we listen to prayers, we gain religious knowledge & at the same time, our vibration is increased. During hearing, there is a transfer of knowledge & if we pay attention, our religious knowledge gets enhanced. The temple or home prayers are truly the first step towards leading a spiritual life. Then, with steadfastness, we can move to the highest levels. It is just like an education system where we start with the pre-primary level & then we can reach the tertiary level. Listening to prayers is a basic step & requires no great effort except a good arrangement & some willpower to start. When listening to prayers, it is important to sense how we are feeling. The greater the feelings, the greater the right connection with God.

The second type of prayer is chanting. In most religions, chanting accompanied by music is very common. When music is added to the prayers, it increases the power of the prayer session & all attendees absorb divine vibrations. I have witnessed people becoming enraptured & ecstatic during beautifully arranged musical prayers- such is the divine energy that can be generated. There is a wide variety of devotional songs available on the internet today & you only have to make a playlist of your own to listen regularly. Chanting prayers can be done alone or in groups- it can also be done aloud or mentally. Both work well, provided the intention to pray deeply is there. Everything depends on the mindset. In all prayers, we also have to understand what we are saying or listening to. Many people pray without understanding

as they have not mastered their religious language! It defeats the purpose of praying when we do not understand its meaning. The translation of common prayers is available on the internet- an effort must be made to read such articles which shall be more than beneficial.

The third type of prayer is called remembering. Here, the devotee is required to think of God as long as possible during the day. This is a practice less performed as it becomes impractical due to our daily material commitments like employment & schooling. But outside of employment & schooling like when travelling, it is possible to practice remembering God. We only have to be conscious & it will surely happen. For example, we can remember God by having a small statue or picture on our desk or car dashboard. The screensaver of our desktop can also be a beautiful divine picture. Of course, this is to be done if there are no procedural restrictions. We can also remember God just before having our meal at the office & school- we only have to offer God our food before eating. This a practice which is of utmost importance for serious seekers of the Truth. Food is divine & is lovingly arranged for us by God through nature. If we don't offer our food to God before eating, then we are committing a sin. You can call on God for help before going to meetings, tests, examinations, presentations or performance appraisal sessions. Truly, if we are conscious of God, then we shall automatically call on Him for all aspects of our lives. Another simple way of remembering God is to see Him everywhere in all creations: a tree, a dog, a butterfly, the ocean, the sunrise, a full moon, a fruit, etc. It is stated in all religions that God is omnipresent, omnipotent & omniscient. Then we have to make an effort to see His intelligence at work everywhere.

Serving the lotus feet of the Lord is the fourth type of prayer. This is rarely practiced today as it is a high-level prayer. It consists of caring for the feet of God. It gives a lot of blessings. In ancient days, in some cultures, it was customary to wash the feet of visitors. This was done with either water or scented oil to relieve the fatigue of the traveller. On a religious level, in Hinduism, this prayer is also performed towards our parents or older relatives to seek their blessings during special prayers. But it is done usually once a year. The feet of the spiritual master can also be worshipped in the same manner. This is usually done on the very auspicious occasion of the Guru Purnima celebration. (full moon prayer dedicated to all Gurus or spiritual masters). In Hinduism, we bow down to touch the feet of the elders, priests & spiritual masters to seek their blessings. It is an act of humility to bow down & the feet are considered to be sacred. It is said that in the time when Lord Krishna was living in India, whenever His devotees used to touch his footprints, they would immediately feel a state of bliss. There is a similar story in Buddhism whereby after His illumination, an astrologer saw the footprint of Lord Buddha. He told him these are the footprints of the King of the world.

Lord Buddha simply told him to stop viewing him as a king. Therefore, it can be safely concluded that the feet are indeed sacred & that the feet of a spiritually elevated person are of great importance. We usually refer to such feet as the lotus feet of God or the lotus feet of the spiritual master. Why lotus, because the lotus is a highly spiritual flower.

The fifth type is prayer is offering prayers to a Deity by way of a statue or picture. There are specific rituals that are associated with prayers of statues & pictures. All these are well elaborated in Hindu sacred texts called the Vedas. It will require the service of a learned priest to perform the prayer as there is a good number of knowledge & mantras for performance. Offerings are also made to the Deities such as lamps, clarified butter, oblations, grains, fruits, incense sticks, etc. In most religions, there is the practice of offering light via a lamp or candle to God. Different deities confer specific blessings to the devotee & when a knowledgeable priest is approached, he can surely guide you towards the fruition of your material desires.

The next prayer is the common way most people use to pray. It is a mixture of simple conversation with God, lighting a lamp, reciting simple mantras, using a string of beads for long recitations, visiting a temple, church or mosque etc. It does not require the attendance of a priest & consists of family traditions & culture transmitted from generation to generation. Different families may have different ways of praying as the ancestral beliefs are not the same. Beliefs play a crucial role in our common prayers- we follow our parent's religious activities without asking questions. Home prayers & temple prayers are limited by nature as they do not inform the devotee of the unlimited potential of a human being.

The seventh mode of praying is very interesting & also uncommon in the modern world due to its impracticality. It is called rendering full-time service to God or to a spiritual master. It is an act of abandoning one's life & to serve a Holy person. It used to happen long ago when Avatars, sages & Holy people were living on Earth. Today, in some religious associations, the rendering of service is made partially possible by rendering service to a Deity- the devotees leave their residence to live at appointed temples. But the original rendering of service is meant for a highly elevated soul or an avatar of God. But we can practice rendering service to human beings by always being kind & helpful. Mother Theresa who spent her whole life rendering service to the poor in India always preached that we should help at least one person every day. "*Help others & God will help you in turn*"- this is how the saying goes. To help genuinely, we need a big heart & true compassion. The bigger our hearts, the more divine we are.

Meditation is the eighth way of praying to God. Although it does not require any ritual or offering, it is a great form of prayer. All meditation techniques serve to connect with the inward God who resides in our hearts- a deep concentration which opens up the doorway to peace & wisdom. The mind is the vehicle of meditation. We are taught how to control our thoughts & how to go deeper inside of us. The duration of a meditation session varies; for beginners, it will be a maximum of fifteen minutes twice per day. In advanced stages, it may reach several hours. Meditation, if properly practiced gives immediate results- we feel light, happy & peaceful. But the effects may disappear after some time as we tend to absorb negative energies from the outside world. So, regular cleansing is necessary. With practice, the effects last longer. The ultimate aim of meditation is to achieve oneness with the Almighty God. It is a process that lasts many years & is achieved after great patience & perseverance. Meditation brings a thorough transformation of the individual & many times it will go unnoticed by ourselves but not by our surroundings. People around you will notice that you are different- you may even receive comments or queries.

The last type of devotion to the Almighty God is certainly the most difficult one & is practiced by rare individuals in this modern world; it is called renunciation. This is the act of surrendering oneself completely to God & to live a solitary life. The amount of social interaction is almost zero as the practitioner has lost the taste for material pleasures & is totally happy with a retired life. Simplicity is the hallmark of renunciation. And as it is rightly said, "*To be spiritual is to be simple.*" Another term to describe a renunciate is a hermit. The modern person will wonder how this is possible because minimum material demands must be met & this is explained by a spiritual phenomenon called self-sufficiency. That is the renunciate has the unshaken trust that his needs shall be met all the time & this is exactly what happens as the all-merciful God will provide everything that is needed for a harmonious life. But what happens when we doubt & are fearful? We always hesitate to cross the limits of a mere mortal life. We then fail to cross over to the spiritual world where peace, happiness, lightness & wisdom are waiting for us. This is what we miss. A renunciate is happy with minimum material comforts in all areas of life & will be able to balance all activities in such ways that whatever is in small amount shall be increased & whatever is in excess shall be decreased. This is the application of the famous Universal Law of the golden median rule given to us by Lord Buddha before leaving this Earth. The rule states that "*we shall neither deprive ourselves nor practice exaggeration.*" When you can do this, it means you are in control of your life. And that is what is required of a spiritual aspirant- to take control, to master the mysteries of life & to become a Master. The key word here is "**master**".

When I make motivational speeches about the nine types of devotion to God, I like to add a tenth one although it is not a prayer towards God. I believe it is as important to perform to expand our consciousness. And that prayer is done towards a person & is called forgiveness. It is stated that "*to forgive is divine.*" In my opinion, it should be categorised as a high-level, non-ritualistic prayer. Forgiving is an extremely difficult task to do for the simple reason that it requires a lot of inner power & wisdom. Very few human beings are ready to devote time to cultivating inner power & wisdom. However, when we are able to forgive, it dissipates a lot of tension & serves to bring harmony back in a relationship or into oneself. Without forgiveness, a delicate & tense situation will continue to disrupt our wellbeing as well as that of all those involved. Inner peace will never be achievable by anyone who is not ready to forgive. Therefore, the choice lies in a decision between fuelling the tensions or forgiving. When we can forgive, then we are effectively elevating our soul to higher levels because this life is full of complications & we shall always be presented with opportunities to apply forgiveness- we should do it without an ounce of hesitation.

Chapter 11

Human Relationships

The softest kind of love is to be patient & forgiving towards all human beings.

The life of a human being is made up of connections- it starts with the family where we identify ourselves with our parents & brothers/sisters. Then, we also have connections with our neighbours, friends & other relatives. Last, but not least, we very often associate intimately with a partner for some time or for our whole life. Adoption of pet animals creates a magnificent bonding and these animals are truly considered as members of our family. It would seem that we cannot live alone. This is precisely the basis of a harmonious life- cooperation & dependence. Nobody is an island & no one will be able to live alone without some kind of dependence. Even if you live alone in a forest, you will depend on the nature around you for sustenance. The Universe operates also in the same manner, based on the collaboration among all its created elements. For example, the oceans cooperate with the Sun to create water evaporation, clouds & rain which are so important for the proper functioning of nature. The pyramid of food ensures that all animals have their basic food requirements, making everything dependent on each other. Spiritually, we say that we are all like beads on the same string.

How do relationships help us in the process of spiritual ascension? Ideally, the family should be the place where we not only obtain physical & emotional nourishment but also spiritual nourishment. The era in which we are living today does not fulfill all of these conditions to a great extent. Our parents do not have sufficient knowledge of the role of a family & how to implement the right upbringing of children- what I wish to say is that the ideal family no longer exists. It is certainly a great responsibility to found a family & to make children- it cannot be a haphazard process of enjoyment of each other's presence/body, sumptuous wedding ceremonies & brightly organised honeymoons! Are you aware that we are "**pushed**" into a married life without the slightest preparation about relationships, how to raise children, etc. I call this trial & error mode & it is quite comparable to the buying of a lottery ticket- *"we'll see what happens."* Human relationships are quite tense today. Last week, I read about a report in my country where it states that the number of weddings is on the decline & that married couples are having only one child. The reason for such a situation is by the time a youngster gets married, that person has probably already gone through three breakups & has had sex with several partners. This is the reality of life today. And stress plays a vital role in deterring people from having a serious relationship.

The family is a place where we no longer benefit from deep learning- it has just become a place of residence. It ought to be a place where we want to get back to when we feel bad so that we can witness the warmth & reassurance of our parents & family members. It must be a place where there is sharing, communication, empathy, joy & caring. The smartphone today, I can safely admit has become another family "**member**" with which we spend more time. And few people are aware of this unbelievable unconsciousness! The fashion & the trend is to say connected as long as possible. I am not against the Internet as it has many advantages. But careful use must be exercised. Human relationships have evolved with time & the culprit is modernism & development. We have successfully created a virtual world in parallel to the already mysterious & difficult world. And we omitted to write the safety operations manual of a virtual world where we have millions of disguised & fake accounts. That is the other side of the coin, at which we don't even cast a glance. When there is stability & the proper energy in all human relationships, then we can be prepared for higher development- otherwise, we spend our time asking questions, remaining in confusion, solving our problems & living an unfulfilled life. Loving, caring & knowledgeable parents will give birth to loving, caring & responsible children, whose DNA at birth will already be at a higher level. It is well known that a pregnant woman must be very careful about her moods & emotions. Why? Simply so as not to affect the baby growing in the womb.

If adults could be conscious that they directly affect the quality of their children by their DNA, then we could create a greater percentage of responsible persons. Our DNA is structured to a good extent by our behaviour. Again, it is a question of Universal Knowledge. Most married couples today face a great deal of tension, up to the point that it is stated that in general, marriage life has both ups & downs. I don't agree with such general statements as we can certainly avoid the setbacks of our lives. We should not accept  such scenarios. Can you imagine the calamities a pregnant woman & her baby are facing if she is constantly being angry or depressed? Or what is the future of kids whose parents are having daily heated discussions? We should not forget that

> *Harmony in human relationships is crucial for society. It begins with cooperation. After harmony is established & sustained for long periods of time, then peace is born*

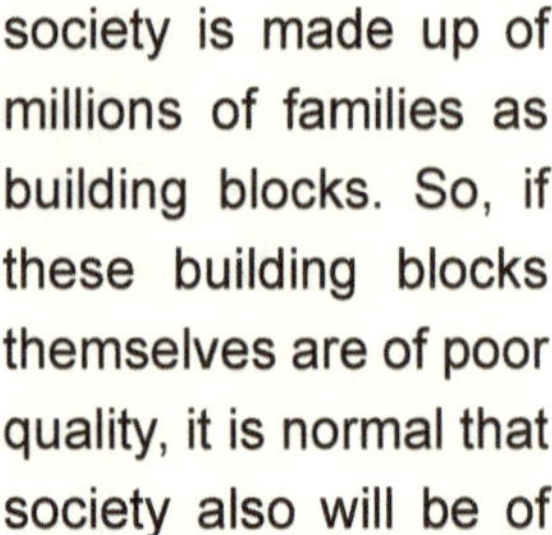

society is made up of millions of families as building blocks. So, if these building blocks themselves are of poor quality, it is normal that society also will be of poor quality. Every adult must take the responsibility to see the bigger picture of the quality of his/her relationships & not limit it to the small family at home. It affects the whole world. We belong both to our small family & to the larger family of the human race. And we should play a responsible role in both families.

Nowadays, human relationships are either solely for selfish motives or are full of stress & pressure. Nobody teaches us of what consists a solid relationship. The first ingredient is trust. This is also a spiritual quality which forms part of another divine quality called openness. When we are able to trust, then a relationship will be at a higher level. But most people find it difficult to trust because of fear & anxiety. Fear & anxiety belong to the same family with the exception that anxiety is more intense than fear. And as long as we fear & cannot trust, we have a miserable married life & contribute also to our partner's misery. The general excuse is that if I trust, then there will be abuse- this is possible but trusting does not mean to be naive & foolish. Spiritually, it is recommended that only those people who can control their emotions should get married or have a partner. And fear as well as anxiety are great negative emotions. When we fear, we are basically living in the future, with

expectations that something bad will happen such as we'll be cheated or there will be a breakup for some reasons. In so doing, the net consequence is that we are wasting the present & by our moodiness, we create a lot of imbalances in the relationship. The solution is simple & it is to adopt the attitude that what will happen will happen, let me enjoy the moment. This is also a spiritual advice, which I believe many of you must be aware of: *"Forget the past & the future, live in the present."*

The next ingredient of a healthy relationship is the capability to forgive your partner for mistakes, offenses, & misgivings. This is also a spiritual dimension which is so difficult to embrace as the easiest solution is to grudge & criticise. We all have flaws in our character & we have to allow someone to learn positive traits & unlearn negative traits. Both are important. Effort & perseverance count a lot. But most of the time, the emotions flare up like gigantic flames & there is no acceptance of the other's faults due to a relentless lack of tolerance & acute impatience. Of course, everything has limits as well but forgiving will settle the scores easily. Very often, we try to shape the person we love in the form that we desire- this is dangerous as most people are not that malleable & are unwilling to change. It is better to accept the circumstances & be tolerant & patient or to communicate why the changes are necessary or last to allow the person to make mistakes even if it means accepting the forthcoming risks.

Having too many expectations from our partners is also a great cause of trouble. Universal Knowledge teaches us that we should drop all expectations in life & take things as they come. But we do exactly the contrary- we keep nurturing expectations & keep getting frustrated. Anger arises from frustrations & then verbal or physical aggression ensues. The starting point is expectations. The latter stems from our ego. We do not choose a partner to exercise control over him/her- it is mostly a sharing.

When you don't have expectations, you are not agitated at all & a calm person rarely makes mistakes. On the contrary, when you have a whole wish list of expectations, you are perpetually in a state of imbalance energetically. And in this state, you are more vulnerable to the slightest changes in the energy of your surroundings & partner. Parents have expectations for themselves, for their children, for their jobs, for the kind of house they will live in and so on. We also wrongly believe that society has expectations of us & we torture ourselves to meet the norms of society. This is done so as not to be an outfit. Again, it is fear at the centre of our actions. There is the absence of freedom & a great deal of energy is spent to conform- there is then no freedom. And a person who is not free cannot be happy. Now I have shown you how everything is intertwined & twisted into each other- this is called the chains of the modern world. Chains become present in our routine due to the absence of higher knowledge & unconsciousness. A spiritual person is an absolutely free person & does not conform to set human rules & regulations- of course, in a positive way and not as a rebel.

Healthy relationships are vital for good physical, emotional & mental health. And to be able to walk on the spiritual path, we need to be in good health or we must get rid of all illnesses. Very often, a spiritual search is started after a great shock by a serious illness, a near-death experience, an intense love affair which breaks up, the death of a close relative or in any other way when the ego gets hurt terribly. But a danger exists in all these negative events as the chances of never being able to turn around the tables also exist. Indeed, it requires a lot of patience, perseverance & support to turn such negative events into a spiritual asset. And divine support is the best door to knock under these circumstances. Relationships are quite fragile & demand constant care & attention as there are always bumps on this road. Negativities such as doubt, jealousy, temptations, pride, ego, misunderstanding, secrecy, evil manipulations & lies are only a few inches behind the door to stir up bad vibrations in any relationship. These can be created by ourselves or by third parties.

There is one relationship on which we don't focus completely or not at all. This is the relationship with our Creator, our origin & source- the almighty God. Our primary relationship is with God, our spiritual Father/Mother. But in the material world, we completely forget this or we are not frequently reminded of this fundamental aspect and we cling desperately to secondary relationships. If we can devote sufficient time to our primary relationship first, then all other relationships will be running smoothly: family, personal, friends & work. We can also be guaranteed to find the right partner at the right time because our loving God wants us to be happy. Because we lack this knowledge, we don't make use of it & the consequences are suffering. And sometimes, if we are aware of this knowledge, we don't have enough trust to implement it. The best way to go about life is to allow life to guide us- then we shall witness its enormous power to be a shining light on our path. Otherwise, we shall be very limited in potential as a human being. The decisive factor here is to recognise our spiritual nature & to turn to the spiritual world for proper guidance. When we try to solve our problems with our own ideas without asking for divine guidance, then these solutions shall not be perfect solutions. As soon as we involve the divine world in the process, the response is different. Sometimes, the divine world puts us under tests to train our patience & resilience.

When we have a close relationship with God, we are guaranteed a happy & peaceful life. However, you should not infer that happiness means material abundance. Spiritual abundance is made up of four elements: peace, lightness, joy

& wisdom. As regards material consumption, there shall always be enough of everything to ensure a harmonious life. Society has set up rigid norms which we follow without asking questions. But it is when we ask the right questions that we start to evolve personally. So, one pertinent question is: do we have to decide to go for a personal relationship with someone to be happy, secure & having our physical, emotional & mental needs to be fulfilled? Can this happiness, peace & security be found by becoming God-conscious? Or do we need to ask why I was born & what is my role on this planet or my role as a human being? Conforming is a great mistake as well as the issue of being chained by cultures, traditions, values, beliefs & superstitions. We have to be free- that is the main purpose. Freedom is the opening up to a wider dimension of life you could never imagine. Of course, freedom goes hand in hand with responsibility- it certainly does not mean liberty towards immoral & unacceptable behaviour.

Another important question that arises is how far are we free in any relationship whether it is parental, friendship or love? That is why you will see many times in history, the seekers of Truth are always lonely persons- but not that lonely as there is always a connection with the spiritual world. The new family is the spiritual family or a wider family made of several members of a community or society itself. But the choice to live alone is indeed a huge one as fear of the unknown, doubts & hesitations shall be formidable obstacles. It is not an easy path. Insults, enemies, rejections & misunderstandings will be present but support from God also will be there- and that is all you need.

Chapter 12

Ordinary Love & Unconditional Love

In his book Memories, Dreams, Reflections, the famous psychotherapist Carl G. Jung stated in the last chapter called Late Thoughts: "*Whatever the learned interpretation may be of the sentence 'God is love', the words affirm the complexio oppositorum (complex of opposites) of the Godhead... I have again and again been faced with the mystery of love and have never been able to explain what it is.*" From this statement, we learn that science is attempting in vain to understand what love is. In the spiritual context, the Universal Knowledge informs us that God is Love, Love is All & All is Love. There is no better way to summarise who God is & what love is. The feeling of love & being loved is indeed one of the greatest we can experience- a distinction must be made here between love & sexual pleasure. Both are not interchangeable terms but evidently one leads to the expression of the other. The need to touch & to have intimacy is very strong when love is declared between two adults & it would seem that the sexual act serves as an emotional bonding between each other. Of course, love is not limited to physical intercourse. It has a much wider dimension than that.

The importance of love in the elevation of one's soul cannot be underestimated. Because love is God and to grow spiritually means to become God-like, which happens in the very late stages. At the end of the spiritual search, the individual soul merges with the Universal soul & has perfected its spiritual ascension. Therefore, we are required to undergo a gradual inner transformation to become more loving towards God, towards oneself & towards all creations. In a nutshell, this is what must be achieved. Our loving Father loves all of us unconditionally even though we are lazy, have little willpower, do not pray enough every day & commit offence & sins regularly. And He forgives us for all that! Can you make the effort to become like Him? I am sure you will be either speechless or say no. That is a terrible mistake- you must believe you can do it. Willpower is nothing but the presence of God by your side to help you. Being a spiritual person does not mean that you shall have absolutely no material life- you will, but it will be a balanced one, neither too much nor too little. Then why should you worry?

In all relationships whether from human to human, from human to animal, from human to plants & objects, from animal to animal & from animal to human, it is obvious that people & animals have the capacity to express affection & care. We call this love to simplify matters. But we have to admit that the capacity to love is greatest in human beings. All feelings have their origin in the heart chakra, found in the middle of the chest. This is why we regularly talk about the heart in romantic & love affairs. Sentences like *"My heart is yours"* or *"Open the door of your heart to me"* are quite common. We have a confirmation here of the origin of feelings but remember we are not referring to the heart organ but the heart chakra. We are given the capacity to express our feelings. Energy is again at the centre of feelings. We are very sensitive to all expressions of care, affection & love. Because love is our essence & our origin.

On Earth, all love is of the ordinary type. I am not in any way trying to downgrade human love but the fact remains that divine love also exists. So, a distinction inevitably arises. The reason behind our love to be ordinary is strictly in relation to the purity of our hearts. The quality of love is directly proportional to the degree of the heart's purity. Since our heart chakra contains a certain level of negativity like fear, guilt, apprehensions, shyness, regrets, resentments and so on, then, obviously the power to love will be according to the state of energy of the heart chakra. You will appreciate that we can be either open to love or closed to love. When we are open, then love flows in our heart & when we are closed, the energy of love is denied access. A person who is submerged by negative emotions will neither be able to love nor will that person attract love towards him, except by a greatly compassionate person who will be able to show care & affection despite the negative situation.

Love is also quite fragile & needs regular nourishment to be kept alive. Conversely, love can be destroyed by sufficient negative energies. Human love is not really true love-it is mostly care, affection, attraction & infatuation. In fact, the condition of living on Earth is dictated by the attraction between the male & female energies which often result in the union of the male & female organs. Such is the basis of the initial creation. With evolution, we are now witnessing the emergence of homosexual love. So, is it love or an attraction/or infatuation? Love amongst humans is said to be conditional love. It happens due to a mutual kind of agreement after the desire to love somebody has been well arisen. In the beginning, you will agree that we are not even aware of the character or behaviour traits of the person- it is mainly a physical attraction due to the appearance & style of the person. Later on, we shall discover the other attributes of the person, which we may like or dislike. Therefore, when conditions are favourable in our view, then we decide to love. It happens over time that the conditions change & then either the love will continue or will be stopped.

Examples of conditions to fall in love are: physical beauty, clothing & hairstyles, perfume, smile, voice, behaviour, wealth, status in society, power, sympathy, pity, help, or "**just like that**", etc. Now, human nature is not fixed & may take sudden deviations from the normal routine, which may cause a disruption in the loving pattern. We also love because our expectations & desires are fulfilled. These physical & emotional gratifications perpetuate the love & may even strengthen it.

Next, the biggest flaw in human love is the power of attachment that is created between two persons. Universal Knowledge teaches us that immense sufferings crop up due to too much attachment. This leads to possessive nature, mistrust & jealousy- all of which are deadly poisons to a healthy relationship. Attachment does not necessarily mean love. It only means that two persons are linked together by emotions, by mutual consent, by family orientation or by duty. Then, where is love? It is extremely difficult to stay in love for a long period- it is easier to stay emotionally connected or bound by family duties. Nevertheless, for those who had the experience of falling in love, it is indeed an amazing one.

On the other hand, we are in the presence of divine love or unconditional love. It is a very rare occurrence on Earth as the name itself implies. It is said that the love closest to divine love is the love of a mother for her newborn baby. For a person to be able to love unconditionally, there must be absolutely no expectations from the loved one. This is a tremendous demand on our bodily system & will require powerful self-control. Very rare souls are daring to work hard to reach that refined stage of human life. But it is such a magnificent experience. When God comes & lives in your heart, the whole perspective of living changes & it changes for the better. Cultivating love & virtue for all, even for our enemies, those who hate us, who despise us & who willingly hurt us, is the way of life we must develop. In this way, we free ourselves from the clutches of conditional love. It is not an easy task but the results are unbelievable

It will take several years to reach the spiritual goal but it can definitely be done in this birth itself, provided you decide firmly this is what you need. Loving unconditionally is about forgetting the dark sides of the other person & to focus only on the bright sides. It means to see love everywhere & in all creations. The reason is the God to whom we pray, is everything: He is the medicine as well as the disease, the youth & the old age, the war & the peace, the confusion & the clarity and everything that you can imagine. We say *"Everything is."* I know this Universal Knowledge will be somewhat destabilising for many of you but this is the way it is. It will take you a lot of inner reflection & pondering to be able to grasp the essence of such words of wisdom; but if you persevere, it will surely happen. Confusion is also an essential component of the spiritual Path. You should not believe that everything becomes clear & insightful in one go- it is a gradual process & you shall be made to remain in confusion for the required duration to grow more. Obstacles on the Path are the greatest teachers. But do we feel comfortable in confusion or do we get thoroughly agitated? What about starting to learn to be undisturbed in the most acute confusion? That is how we progress- by overcoming ourselves & all that is untrue, unreal & illusionary. Then the bright light of God will shine.

Unconditional love is the highest form of love & will require a superior form of ourselves to be reborn in order to be able to implement. An open heart will be the aim. In an open heart, there is enormous compassion, empathy, gentleness, kindness, help & responsibility. These soft skills must be developed purposefully

& with a strong intention. Then, all the knots in the heart shall be untied. Our heart does not really want God- this is a fact. The simplest & appropriate way to cultivate the qualities of an open heart is to start a process of monthly charity. You are all aware of the saying: service to mankind is service to God. If you become conscious that a small part of your monthly revenue can be set aside to help the poor & needy, then you are already making the first steps towards a God-like nature. Of course, charity will not be the only method to grow spiritually but it is a vital component of the elevation of one's soul. What happens when we adopt charity is that we send the message to the Universe that we are not only conscious of our small family but of the whole human race. God loves this mindset & will shower loads of blessings to all those who go out of their way to help the poor & the needy. A word of caution is worthwhile here: do charity not to please yourself & not to derive pride & grandeur from your actions. I have seen people become so entangled in charity just to satisfy their ego! This is a serious mistake. Simplicity is the hallmark of spirituality. We should not boast about our charity actions. There is an important rule of the Universe which must be satisfied to bring harmony in our lives: it is to understand that the amount of receiving & giving must be carefully balanced. So, you need to sit with yourself & find out whether you are more in the receiving or giving mode; then you can modify your course of action to re-establish the equilibrium. When we give more, we shall feel bad as we will certainly feel that our environment is abusing our assistance. When we are receiving more, then we are probably in the greed & selfish mode. Both are unstable conditions & need to be rectified.

Chapter 13

How to Manifest Your Thoughts

> *Living restless, without depth or meaning, life is insignificant & one is prone to make mistakes.*
> *(Chinese Proverb)*

At the time of creation, the Eternal God created a self, which is a Higher Self compared to us. This Higher Self is the Universal Spirit or the Cosmic Mind. Then this spirit started creation because the basic function of spirit is to think & create. Human beings are made exactly as the original spirit but with diminished capabilities. A physical body also is given to human beings. This is how it happens at the origin. Given that we are endowed with a mind, then we are also capable of thinking & creating. And of course, intelligence also is required to be able to create. The highest intelligence is God & if you look well around you, you will see intelligence at work everywhere. There is also a huge difference between divine creation & human creation.

Divine creation is instantaneous & requires no preliminary material to start with. Divine energy is at the root of all creations whether living or non-living. The soul is a microscopic spark of the Eternal light of God. Human beings need raw materials to create- to be exact, we are assembling or transforming existing materials into new objects. For instance, we crush rocks & make bricks to build houses. We have not & will never reach the stage of

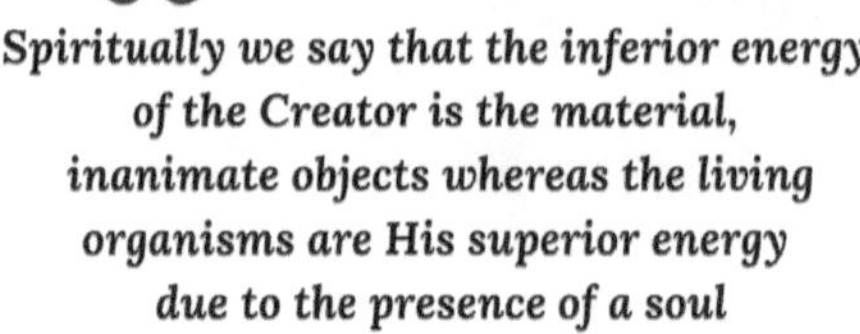

creating a rock from nothing. Because at the time of creation, there was absolutely nothing in existence except the Eternal God- it was pure emptiness. At this point, I wish also to inform you that we don't invent anything. By divine intervention, selected persons are made to discover something which God has already planned for us. And the big plan is rolled over as time passes by. Because you see, the plan has a start & a finish. And to gradually end a plan, there must be gradual degradation & then the final destruction.

So, we can think, assemble & transform matter by the use of various processes. We all have our personal level of vibration based on our degree of personal evolution after a series of successive births & deaths. The more evolved we are, the higher our inner energy, the higher our intelligence & the higher our capability to create. I am using the term create but as I have informed earlier, we are not creating in the absolute meaning. We mostly make use of our intelligence to create and our internal energy stays at the same level. With experience & research, our intelligence increases & as such, we give rise to improved versions of the same creation or new objects. The act of manifesting thoughts is done at an energetic level. Neither intelligence is required nor the use of processes of transformation.

As we increase the vibration of our personal energy through different spiritual practices of internal cleansing & expansion of our consciousness, then we are able to manifest our thoughts & wishes. But here again, we are not manifesting in the same way as God created the Universe. We are simply able to materialise our desires. There are also different stages of manifestation & it varies with the level of consciousness & energy we have reached. Our vibration can be measured in terms of hertz just as in the physical world. There is a span of frequencies which is attributed to the human plane & another span for the divine world. From this perspective, you will find that we have just described the existence of a ladder of available frequencies in nature. And the process of elevating our soul or of self-realisation is more precisely the ascension of this ladder.

On the human plane, as we increase our internal energy, we shall be able to manifest simple desires like getting a job or someone gifting you an apple. When we cross over to the divine plane, we are able not only to materialise desires but also to create material objects out of nothing. An example here is of a famous saint in India, by the name of Sri Satya Sai Baba, who was able to materialise scented ash in his hand to distribute to devotees. In other cases, we have stories of yogis who have the ability to perform astral projections- that is to travel to another location by materialising & dematerialising the body. I am stating this as an example to make you step into the world of heightened psychic abilities. These arise due to the higher level of internal energy & due to the expansion of the consciousness. In other words, superconsciousness is a phenomenon that some people can exhibit after a great deal of personal internal work on their energies, several years of meditation & living in solitude. So as not to confuse you further, I will state a few common psychic abilities: clairvoyance, clairaudience, clairsentience & the reading of thoughts. There are other complex psychic abilities which an elevated soul can perform.

The materialisation of thoughts seems to be a great feat to achieve & will always attract people to the spiritual Path only for this reason. Fortunately, the loving God knows who is humble enough to handle such powers & therefore, they are not automatically granted due to the possibility of misuse. And of course, if ever there is misuse, there is also punishment because we should not forget that our loving God is also the God of Punishment. He does not punish in an absolute term but only after a procedure or law has been transgressed. So, humility & responsibility play a crucial role after such psychic powers become manifest. Power without responsibility whether in matters of spirituality, politics, business & finance will always fail to deliver high-quality results. People have always been & will always be attracted to any kind of power. When the ego is present & gets mixed with power, this is where abuse of power will begin. Corruption also will be present due to greed fuelled by power. And in such instances, spiritually, we call these persons demons. Mythology is full of stories where people have misused their powers & have ultimately been killed by God. One such famous example in Hinduism is the demon Ravana who was slain by Lord Rama.

Our thoughts can be both positive & negative- we are all aware of this. But for a person who is aspiring to higher levels of internal energy & consciousness, it is highly advisable to think twice if negative thoughts still persist in the mind. The reason is that negative thoughts & harmful desires will also get manifested! This is a dangerous situation. That is why such energies arise only after a thorough self-control of the mind has been achieved. When our energy is not elevated, thoughts are also dangerous because the karmic reaction is ever-present. Karma says "*in whatever way you act, you will reap back a corresponding reaction.*" Behind all actions, there are thoughts. As indicated, even at a lower level of life, it is imperative to control our thoughts. It is recognised that excessive negative thoughts can cause illnesses as well as severe mental complications. Now, if you add to that a karmic effect, then we have to be very effective in the management of our mind.

Another important element in the realisation of thoughts & wishes, irrespective of our levels of energy is the intensity of the thoughts. You can think of thoughts as flames which we generate from our mind. If a thought is like the flame of a matchstick, it will not be able to cut through a piece of steel. Whereas if it is like the flame of a cutting torch, then the steel will not be able to resist. How do we add power to our thoughts? It is by having a strong mind & believing very strongly that this desire is really what we want. Then, there shall be materialisation. This is logical as the Universe which is the receptor of our thoughts should be very clear about what we want. If there is the slightest doubt or if the thoughts are not consistent, then the Universe is confused & she does not act for you. To be able to have consistent thoughts will require a well-trained mind. And the rectification of the mind is called the cultivation of the Higher Self, nothing else. Not prayer, not fasting, not regular pilgrimage to holy places, not daily visits to temples and not regular celebrations of festivals. All these show an outward emotional manifestation of a personal identification or a set of beliefs. Whereas the Path to God is an inner transformation, a change of vital energy, a cleansing of the heart & mind, a non-stop positive behaviour, pure intentions and selflessness. Do you notice the basic difference? It is a question of inward & outward concern. The modern physical world emphasizes the outward tangible events & phenomena whereas the spiritual world deals with the inward intangible processes.

You will be surprised to learn that most people don't really know what they want specifically. Erratic thoughts about the same issue are very common because there is insufficient control of the mind. Spiritually it is said that we should also know what we don't want. Very few people give this issue the required importance. For a thinking process to be complete, we need to know what we want & what we don't want. Then the process becomes clearer. The thing is if we leave space for a greater number of possibilities in our thinking exercise, then the Universe will not be able to decide which wishes to grant to us. As an example, if we ask to pass our examinations, it is vague as anything above 50% marks means passing. Then if we say we wish to pass our examinations with at least 65% marks. Now it's getting more specific. But it is still comprised of several possibilities. We should not hesitate to say "*I want 75% marks.*" This one is very clear & there is only one possibility.

It is also important to note that at a certain level of human energy, it will be necessary to add some of our input in terms of efforts. For this level, the best way to go about materialisation of thoughts is to ask God to guide our intelligence & mind about what we must do to reach our objectives. This works very well as we are open to making efforts & nature loves people who work hard. So, in this way, the chances are greater. Another issue about the fulfillment of wishes is that we should never use negative words like "**not**" in our requests. For example, we should not say "*Oh God, please do not make me fail my tests.*" The conversation with the divine world should always be positive, and clear of doubts & suppositions. One less-used mode of asking for wishes is by asking God to give us what is best for us according to our circumstances. This is done by people of a certain wisdom & who have understood very well how the Universe operates. In order to do this, we must first have a superior inner energy to trust that God will give us what we need & secondly, we must be free from greed. A great way of describing wishes & desires in the spiritual context is to state that desires are equivalent to a ladder which has a start & no end.

I will conclude this chapter with a very special instruction from the divine world with regard to the effective management of desires. It is said that the desireless person is the happiest person. The saying goes further by assuring that the bliss of the absence of desires cannot be compared even to the state of being the wealthiest person on Earth. To be desireless involves the intentional conditioning of the mind that we are satisfied with what we are & with what we have. This is what we should aim for in life instead of climbing the ladder of desires & running the risk of being always restless. A restless mind is a great suffering- we are not meant for that. The best gift to our brain is to have only a few thoughts during the waking state & to have absolutely no thoughts during our daily meditation sessions. When the brain has little or no thoughts, then it shall operate at its full potential. This has to be clearly understood.

Chapter 14

The Techniques of Kriyas for Self-Realisation

> *When you are always positive, you open the doors to the great treasures hidden in the depths of the subconscious. (Chinese Proverb)*

In the previous chapters, I have elaborated on the different methods, behaviours & knowledge necessary to embark fruitfully on the spiritual path to reach the highest possible state of human consciousness, that is self-realisation. It is also called illumination, enlightenment or samadhi. Indeed, it is not a simple process but with careful discipline & patience, we can witness a totally new way of life. Many people haven't even heard of the term self-realisation or enlightenment, believing that human life is limited to the variegated experiences of the physical world & that there does not exist anything beyond the material plane. This is a great illusion & also mostly a dream in the waking state. We need to wake up!

Kriyas are methods which allow the practitioner to elevate the consciousness in a powerful & direct way. It is performed by persons in good health only. People with high blood pressure, heart issues, lung problems, handicaps, etc & who are on regular medication should abstain from practicing kriya. All kriya exercises require careful supervision by an expert in order to get results. A person who practices kriyas is called a kriyaban. So, what is a kriya? It is a set of specific, high-level breathing exercises which are very ancient and which have been divinely given to yogis to practice to perfect their lives. Then, in turn, they have transmitted this knowledge to other students & the process is continuing till now. Some of the kriyas are simple & can be performed by novices but as the taste for kriyas increases, the practice of higher kriyas will require follow-up by an expert. Every individual is unique and will have a different pace of progress which must be closely monitored. Dangers exist in the practice of kriyas especially related to excess zeal & over-practice. The reason is that the results of kriyas are quick & sometimes explosive depending on the person. And if the person's ego cannot resist the impulse to overindulge in the practices, then negative effects will be perceived such as dizziness & laziness.

The experience with kriyas is absolutely incredible. It makes the kriyaban become aware of the reality of existence & the beauty of increased energies inside the body. The different states which are felt cannot be described by words- it has to be lived. All the energy centres of the body get a gradual boost or sometimes a sudden boost with the effect that the sensations are huge. When the centres in the brain are activated, the experience is mind-blowing. However, the practitioner should not be greedy about these experiences as the sole aim is to transcend peacefully to the higher states & certainly not in an arrogant way. The higher you climb, the greater the risks of falling- this is well known. And when you fall from a greater height, the consequences are greater & sometimes irreversible. This is very important to understand as there is the existence of a great risk on the way to

God: it is the development of the spiritual ego. The complication arises because when we ascend to higher levels, the ego also increases in power. And if in parallel, we don't make the efforts to transcend the ego, then the consequences are negative & contrary to what is expected of a fruitful spiritual attainment.

Kriya is also called a yoga technique; that is, it helps the practitioner to achieve oneness with God. It also makes use of yoga postures such as the perfect & lotus postures for performing the breathing exercises. The results of effective kriya allow to witness the internal light of each chakra. Kriya also uses our seven main chakras from the root chakra (base of the spine or coccyx) to the crown chakra (top of the skull) to expand our consciousness. The other five chakras are the sacral chakra (just below the navel), the solar plexus (middle of the rib cage), the heart chakra (centre of chest), the throat chakra (throat) & the third eye (middle of eyebrows intersection). Our chakras have two aspects: one is internal & the other is external. The inner aspect is the light or vibration of the chakra, which when increased, will help the consciousness to be directed towards God. The outer aspect of a chakra is to provide physical, bodily sustenance to the organs which are situated close to it. Kriya considers the spinal column as a hollow tube in which energy flows & it is not a coincidence that most of the chakras are situated on the spinal column. Our chakras can absorb both negative & positive energies- they may be considered as discs which are rotating at their respective locations. They also have specific colours attributed to them. Sometimes, when the individual is faced with enormous stress, diseases & personal problems, these chakras become blocked. The feelings shall then be of intense laziness, difficulty in performing our daily tasks & the inclination to stay lying in bed. Such are the huge effects of blocked chakras. But when each chakra is cleansed, the individual feels normal again.

Reiki (Japanese natural healing technique) also uses the chakras for self-healing & to heal others. I have personally used Reiki to heal a lot of people & it is a beautiful experience. The explanation of the cause of all diseases is due to an imbalance of internal energy. That is what happens even before symptoms start to appear. And our energy affects our body & our body also affects our energy. When our chakras are in good health, our body also is in good health. All are interconnected & affect the functioning of each other. Kriya exercises add to our Universal Knowledge due to further information on how our body functions & inform us of the existence of other chakras. Such chakras are the medullar, fontanelle & bindu chakras found in our skull. And the

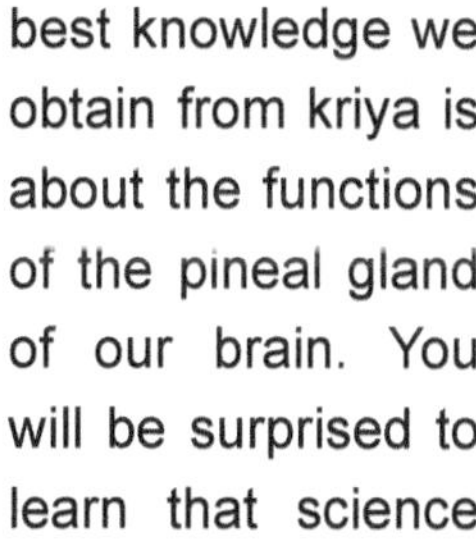

> *The pineal gland is essentially a spiritual gland that is dormant for everybody except for those who are practicing high-level exercises such as meditation, yoga & kriya.*

best knowledge we obtain from kriya is about the functions of the pineal gland of our brain. You will be surprised to learn that science has not yet discovered what is the function of this gland. Great ancient masters have been fully aware of its function for many centuries. When the pineal gland becomes activated, our energy, senses & body function at a heightened level. Now you are aware that there are spiritual parts in our body & that actually we are much more evolved than we think. This unconsciousness arises due to ignorance & due to the concentration on the outer aspects of our body. And as I have pointed out several times, ignorance is a really dangerous situation.

Kriya works in the same way as Reiki initiations in that there are different levels attributed. There are eight basic kriya techniques which are available to those enrolling on a beginner's level. Kriya is best performed early morning on an empty stomach. You will note here that just like yoga & meditation, spiritual practices are performed early in the morning. But in the modern world, few people are keen to wake up early. Kriya is quite complex in terms of procedures even at the beginner level & must be well understood before full practice in terms of recommended repetitions. After you have fully mastered the technical aspects of each kriya exercise, then only you can start by planning for a daily kriya routine composed of the eight exercises. All this will require time, dedication & discipline- the basic qualities of a serious student. Kriya is to be practiced in a joyful mood. Then the results are best. Kriya has very noticeable side effects. This happens by overindulgence.

Kriya is a very serious spiritual practice & should not be treated lightly. It may change your life drastically. Normally, it is not meant for trial only but for starting & persevering until the final results are obtained. There are numerous techniques involved & it is not the purpose of this book to teach kriya. Kriya is practiced with the guidance of a kriya expert. I have practiced up to a certain level as an experience. For knowledge & personal experience, I will share with you two exercises, not for the sake of practicing but for knowledge's sake.

The first technique is called kechari. To perform this, you must sit in either siddhasana or lotus posture. Then with your clean hand, you will need to gently push your tongue upwards inside your throat. It is not easy to do. It will not go in the throat during initial trials- it will tend to slip back into its normal position. After persisting, you will finally achieve progress. Then you will try to push your tongue gently upwards in the pharynx. The tip of the tongue will press against a soft point inside the pharynx. At this point, you can close your eyes, relax & enjoy any experience you get. If you feel any discomfort like pain or excessive salivation, you should stop & try the next day. This kriya should be done only once a day in the beginning. As you see, this may seem an awkward practice but it gives great results. After some time of regular practice, you will feel a strange but good feeling of peace in your head. Arriving at this point, you can do up to three times a day. You will know you are performing it correctly when you feel absolutely no discomfort & when you feel that the tongue is naturally in its position in the pharynx.

The second kriya is called guiding the light in the brain. This one is fairly simpler than the first kriya. For this one also, you sit either in siddhasana posture or lotus posture. Then, you imagine light is entering through the top front of your skull into your brain. After this, very slowly, raise your chin by a few millimetres as if to guide the light in a specific region called the cerebellum. At this point, if your level of energy is appropriate, you shall witness a great light on your forehead. You can gaze at it for a few seconds, lower down the chin again & start over again. The process can be repeated five times in the beginning. You will certainly not see any light at the beginning of this practice but this should not discourage you from continuing. After successful mastery of the technique, you can go for more repetitions until one hundred & eight repetitions are reached. It will defeat the purpose of going up to one hundred & eight repetitions at the beginning when you are not seeing any light. The light has to come first, then the number of repetitions is increased.

After six to twelve months of practicing basic kriyas, then you can move to higher kriyas if you feel that kriya is what you need in your life. Regular practice of the basic kriya will completely change the awareness you have of yourself & of others. You will also start to view your surroundings differently. Enjoyment of the spiritual dimension is the purpose of kriya. Lightness, peace & joy are the direct sensations after mastery of the beginner's kriya yoga. These feelings will certainly make you develop a passionate commitment towards kriya & pursue it at higher levels. The role of the higher kriya is to remove all obstacles that exist in the heart & which prevents the practitioner from ascending to higher levels of consciousness. Moods & emotions reside in our hearts- they are great barriers to self-realisation. Higher kriyas will enable you to develop what is called emotional maturity. You shall then enjoy a healthy relationship with yourself, your emotions & your instincts- the common man doesn't show sufficient control over these aspects during a whole lifetime. As you perfect your higher kriya techniques, you will also become more God-conscious. All your actions will be done in the remembrance of God.

Chapter 15

Elements of a Positive Lifestyle

> *Fire clings to the wood to keep burning. We also have to cling to something to keep our brightness. That something is the internal light in our hearts.*
> *(Chinese Proverb)*

Many of us have heard the saying: *"Think positive & act positive."* It is really a great saying but what are we supposed to do by the application of this procedure? And most important also, what are we supposed not to do? In a previous chapter, I have emphasized on the process of unlearning as compared to learning. The same line of thought applies to the realm of a positive lifestyle. I strongly believe that  mere sayings & speeches do not have a far-reaching impact on our lives, for the simple reason that we must be explained why we are to adopt a particular behaviour. Even after explaining, that does not mean we are guaranteed that the person who has received a spiritual piece of advice will start its implementation. This life is of dual aspect- everything that exists also has its opposite. Therefore, suffering & negativities must have their opposites, which are liberation & positivities respectively.

In order to start adopting a positive lifestyle, we must first of all become conscious that this is what we want. As soon as this happens, the Universe will definitely start sending us the required help. Everything starts at the level of the mind, the creator of thoughts, ideas & manifestations. The next step is to believe strongly in what you are doing. This relates to the power of intentions. If our intentions are meagre & of low intensity, the chances of getting started are minimal. After starting, it is now crucial to keep going with sustained patience & perseverance. These two qualities are of utmost importance in the realisation of any project, be it spiritual or personal. We should not adopt the attitude of a quitter or else, we shall never meet our objectives. In order to facilitate your approach to a positive lifestyle, I have regrouped the tasks as well as categorised them in terms of the degree of ease of implementation, viz, easy, intermediate & difficult. This is a general line of thought & will not necessarily apply to all of you in the same manner. Some people are better at difficult tasks whereas others prefer simple tasks. But overall, this is a drop-list of what can constitute a healthy lifestyle.

EASY STEPS TO A POSITIVE LIFESTYLE:

- **Smile more often to yourself & to others.** This simple task will attract a lot of positive vibrations in you. Try to smile even if you are going through a hard time.
- **Exercise physically for fifteen minutes every day excluding weekends.** By exercise, I am not referring to fashion exercises like going to a gym, Zumba dancing and so on but to walking, jogging, cycling or swimming. The intensity must be high enough for your heart to beat strongly. The scope of any exercise is to feel good & motivated after the session. We should not feel tired & have painful muscles. Today, the fashion is about pumped-up muscles, six-pack abdominals, etc stimulated by the use of chemicals. Again, it is a

question of intelligent choice- you don't need to prove to yourself & to others that you can do two hours of workout in the gym.

- **Drink water regularly up to one litre per day.** A good hydration level prevents us from being dehydrated, which can cause fatigue.
- **Stay outside more often than indoors.** We need fresh air, oxygen & sunlight for a healthy body. Artificial light can cause disruptions in our wellbeing. It is recommended to have a morning or late evening sunlight exposure at least ten minutes per day. Every week, spend at least forty-five minutes in nature. But do it without your smartphone. Alone is best. Observe nature & its plants & animals. Nature is our real home.
- **Say very regularly "thank you" for minor things.** We don't need to wait for exceptional things to express our gratitude to God & to others. Many people believe a **"thank you"** note is only for great occasions. Examples of situations are: when waking up, to thank for a good night's sleep; before eating your meals; for a glass of water which quenches your thirst; for coming back home safely every day after work or school; for being in good health; for having a job.
- **Help one person every day.** It is not financial help only that counts. Any kind of little help is most beneficial- it shows we have a clean heart. But don't help tactically to obtain favours later on. This is selfishness. While driving, you can give way to drivers in difficulty; you can open the door for someone; offering a cookie or sweet is a nice & cheap gesture.
- **Holding hands, hugging, holding the arms, patting the shoulders.** This does not apply only to lovers. Parents & children, close friends can also do this. Human beings adore warmth & attention. But care must

be taken not to convey the wrong message or to take advantage of such closeness. Those who have been in love know the feelings of being close by simple touch gestures- I am not referring to sex here but to highlight the importance of human warmth.

- **Repeat daily positive affirmations which start with "I am":** Positive affirmations when recited regularly have a positive impact on our psychic & emotional states. Remember that words even internal ones are made up of sound energy & our body is both a transmitter & receiver of energy. Thus, positive affirmations will serve to upgrade our wellbeing. It is the same process as in the recitation of mantras in Hinduism, Buddhism & other religions. Examples of such affirmations are:

  - I am a child of God.
  - I am Spirit.
  - I am eternal.
  - I am positive.
  - I am fearless.
  - I am gentle & compassionate.

You can devise your own positive affirmations based on what you know about your weaknesses & what you want to achieve.

INTERMEDIATE STEPS TO A POSITIVE LIFESTYLE

- **Avoid at all costs judging & criticising people:** This is very common nowadays and spiritually, we say we must learn to control our speech. Because speech is sacred: we often forget this very important aspect. Very often, in groups, clubs, religious associations & the office, we find subgroups being formed & the idea is to talk behind the back of others.

- **Pray for at least ten minutes morning & evening:** This aspect is regularly practiced in great haste or is almost inexistent due to lack of time or focus. Prayer is a simple way to have divine support. The fast pace of life makes us concentrate more on material issues rather than devotional issues.

- **Control the amount you eat:** It is said that the wise have full control over the taste function. Eating for taste is considered a sin. Eating regularly in between meals will lead to diseases & obesity. The problem is we have a much larger variety of fast foods & snacks available today. We also have services of delivery at home, which makes life a lot easier.

- **Do not eat until you feel your stomach is full:** We should leave the table feeling just a little hungry but not completely satiated & burping. The stomach is not an organ to be pleased, neither is the tongue. The world as a global village is giving us the opportunity to taste meals of many cultures under one roof called a food court. It is very tempting & certainly difficult to resist but efforts are necessary to eat properly.

- **Eat more vegetables & fruits if you are non-vegetarian:** This is mandatory for the proper functioning of the body. Lack of fibre from fruits & vegetables can cause constipation as well as serious intestinal troubles. I see many adverts on big television channels promoting the intake of five fruits & vegetables per day. Vegetarian food is digested quicker than non-vegetarian food- typically in two hours less. Our digestive system is like a factory and it will need both rest & maintenance. Eating every five to six hours is a good average whereas eating every two to three hours is not recommended. Also do not have dinner after 20h30 as you will still have digestion in your stomach while sleeping. 7 pm is a good time for dinner.

- **Reduce drastically or stop the consumption of toxic products:** Alcohol, cigarettes & drugs are not needed by our body. These are consumed as fashion or ignorance & for pleasurable sensations. Canned foods or any foods which are preserved by chemicals also constitute a risk. Our liver is the organ which will be impacted by toxic products since its function is to eliminate toxins in our blood. If you make it work hard, then it can develop silently serious illnesses after several years.

- **Perform a one-weekly fasting to promote better health:** Here, I am not referring to religious fasting but to a scientific one. It consists of depriving the stomach of solid food as long as allowable by your health & willpower. You may drink warm water to activate the elimination of toxins & waste from your body. Our digestion is like a fire and with time its capacity decreases. It can be rekindled by regular fasting. Take care not to eat a super meal just after fasting! Keep it for a few days later. It is recommended to have a light meal when breaking a fast.

- **Sleep and wake up at regular hours:** Our body has an internal clock which is set by our habits. Discipline is what our body needs. When discipline is absent, the mind is happy as it is nourished by our senses but our soul is confused by too many material concerns. It is discipline which sends positive vibes to the soul.

- **Control your moods:** You will find that moodiness is a cause of lowered energy and it adversely affects your wellbeing as well as that of your surroundings. What you don't realise is that you have the power to control & stop it just as you have the freedom of choosing to be moody at will. So, it is a question of choice but the easy way around is to sulk & be moody for several hours or days. This affects your internal energy, your chakras & your health.

- **Be loving & caring rather than emotional:** There is a huge difference between caring & loving. To be emotional means to absorb all the energies about a situation. When you are loving, you don't need to absorb external energies. Control of emotions is a spiritual instruction as emotions disturb our vital energy, hence our balance as well. To achieve this, you must train your mind to be calm. To learn to be calm, you must be in silence regularly.

- **Control of sexual activity:** It will be tough to control such an activity which gives the highest pleasure to the body. But when you learn that sex depletes your vital energy, then probably you will think twice. Spiritual aspirants who want to reach the higher stages of consciousness are recommended to refrain from sex. The sexual energy which is locked in the coccyx chakra at the base of the spine can then move upwards to nourish the higher chakras one by one until the energy reaches the sixth chakra, i.e. the third eye. When our consciousness is at this level, we are no longer affected by the material world. When our consciousness is on sex, we are blocked at the coccyx chakra, very far away from a spiritual life.

DIFFICULT STEPS TO A POSITIVE LIFESTYLE

- **Stop worrying:** You will find that worrying is our second nature. It is as simple to worry as to breathe. Such is the nature of the conditioned mind. If you think about it carefully, you will conclude that nine out of ten of our worries just never materialise. But you cannot stop yourself from worrying. Worry affects your health & symptoms will persist until you remove the worries from your system. It causes insomnia, depression, acid reflux, weight loss, hair loss, lateness in menses, skin problems, etc.

- **Wake up between four & five in the morning every day:** The spiritual vibration present two hours before sunrise is the best which exists every twenty-four hours. So, why should we waste this valuable & auspicious time? I am asked regularly: *"But what will I do at this time?"*. I have provided in this book many tasks that can be done at this particular time. The first challenge is to get started & the second is to keep going. And all will depend on how well you use your mind for setting up a positive lifestyle.

- **Always believe in yourself:** This is a crucial aspect of our self-development as a strong belief is like a catalyst to the mind. Sensational jobs can be done by only thinking positively. Again, if you have low self-esteem, you are informing your mind that you cannot perform the task at hand. And your mind will set an enormous obstacle to your projects.

- **Everyday develop patience, perseverance & resilience:** These three qualities are fundamental to be able to go through life undisturbed. I can assure you that life will give you enough opportunities to develop them. And it is only repeated challenges which build up a strong mind. A comfortable life will never push you out of your limits to make you discover your hidden potential. Resilience means that you do not allow life to wear you down- so that each time you fall, you gather enough energy & internal resources to lift yourself either alone or with external support.

- **Become bold & fearless:** Nature favours the bold & fearless ones. You just boldly make the first moves & witness how life gives you the additional required support. Very often, we make the mistake of waiting for life, something or someone to trigger that "**kick**" to start! But if we dare to make the first step, we shall be much better off.

- **Meditate for fifteen minutes, twice a day if you are a beginner:** To meditate, does not mean to look for a renowned centre where a famous spiritual person resides or gives meditation tuition. It is simply sitting on your own in silence & to be with yourself. Just ensure your back is straight & let the Universe guide you- it can be felt after regular practice. You should not believe that you are alone. The Universe is a Cosmic Mind which is observing us at all times- you can think of it as a gigantic electromagnetic net which envelopes the whole creation. And that divine electromagnetism has the capability to connect with us, receive our own electromagnetic emissions (which are our thoughts) & transmit other electromagnetic waves to us. A higher level of electromagnetism means higher intelligence, just like a more intelligent person has more electromagnetic activity in the brain. This has already been proven by science.

- **Adopt the Golden Median Rule:** It states that in all our activities, we should neither deprive ourselves nor be in excess, that is we need to avoid minima & maxima. This has been gifted to humanity by Lord Buddha. He attained illumination after so many hard trials, up to starving himself & becoming skinny. Then, one day when he saw a musician who was tuning his violin, he got the final illumination- that all this time, he was striving too hard to achieve his aim. He was not aware that he had only to step back & be less daunting in his practice to achieve enlightenment. So, too much & too little are both harmful. We need to balance everything. And it is only the controlled mind which will allow us to do this. An uncontrolled, conditioned, polluted & disobedient mind will lead us away from a healthy lifestyle. Verily, that is what great masters teach us.

- **Our daily behaviour must be carefully monitored:** Behaviour is intricately connected to our karma. We reap as we sow- such is the basic principle of the Law of Karma. As soon as we get a physical body, we are subject to this law. In order to behave correctly, we should purge both our mind & heart. This requires knowing who we are currently & who we must become. Sometimes, the truth is invisible & even hard to admit: this is the condition of human life. One effective way of progressing along this path is to introspect our daily actions every day before going to sleep. Analysing ourselves like this will lead to understanding ourselves in a deeper sense. Then, we shall be cautious every time the same situation arises. That cautiousness is one of the pillars of a spiritual life.

- **See love everywhere:** Human nature is sometimes loving, sometimes harsh. It can never be 100% loving nor 100% harsh. At this stage, we then have two distinct choices. We can focus only on the negative aspects of life & be miserable or we can focus only on the positive traits & live a better life. What is best, we can be wise & accept that both are the same sides of the same coin. Being wise is a terrific objective in life. Love is God & God is love. Developing your consciousness to see God in a worm, in the rain, in the moon, and in a difficult situation, will transform you.

- **Love yourself:** We develop love of ourselves- not in an egoistic & proud way but in the absolute sense. No one teaches us this simple lesson. When you can love yourself, it means you are completely satisfied with the way you are & also satisfied with what you possess. Such a person is undisturbed & not fighting about anything in life. This important message is also transmitted to the divine world & makes you earn a lot of points in the divine's eyes. Being satisfied also helps to keep desires away & thus the chances of frustrations are less. When you love yourself well, you shall be able to be more loving towards others- people will be more attracted to you. Your understanding of others will take a leap; because you are more loving, you are also more forgiving. Then, your personal relationships will be better.

Chapter 16

Masculine & Feminine Energies

The study of nature is the intercourse with the Highest Mind. (Chinese Proverb)

The world we live in is essentially made up of forces, contrary to the common belief that it is made up of only objects & things. There are invisible forces acting everywhere without us being conscious of them. We have discovered a few of them & the most significant one is the gravitational pull between all the planets. And in physics, we have learnt that forces can do work or actions, that is, they cause a transfer of energy. We can also state that everything is energy- from the God who created the Universe to all that exists. This is because living organisms derive their energy from the energy of the soul & non-living matter is made up of protons, neutrons & electrons which are packets of energy. The transformation of energy is the basis of creation & the basis of life.

The Eternal God has both inner masculine & female energies, equally balanced. Both energies have a spiritual aspect- the masculine energy is called the Yang & the female energy is called the Ying. The Ying & the Yang are famous in Chinese Feng Shui & serve to balance the energies of a person & his house or office. The masculine energy is the leadership power which is unleashed to start the process of building the Universe. It is a very strong assertive energy which has an equally extraordinary decisive nature. That is to say, it is a starter. Masculine energy is related to goal orientation & to make things happen. The common masculine traits are assertiveness, strength, confidence, courage & independence. To be assertive means to be confident & direct in expressing thoughts & needs. Independence means that there is a high degree of self-reliance & the ability to take care of oneself. Masculine energy also means boldness & the ability to confront fear & adversity. Confidence is related to a strong self-assuredness to make decisions. And other traits associated with masculine energy are protectiveness, competitive spirit, ambition & logical reasoning. You should not consider masculine energy as dominating & oppressive but as empowering & supportive. These are the basic functions of masculine energy. At a spiritual level, wisdom is termed as a masculine energy. It is a highly prized characteristic which consists of a particular type of intelligence, which is used to understand the Great Laws of the Universe, to understand oneself & to understand others. Wisdom, as

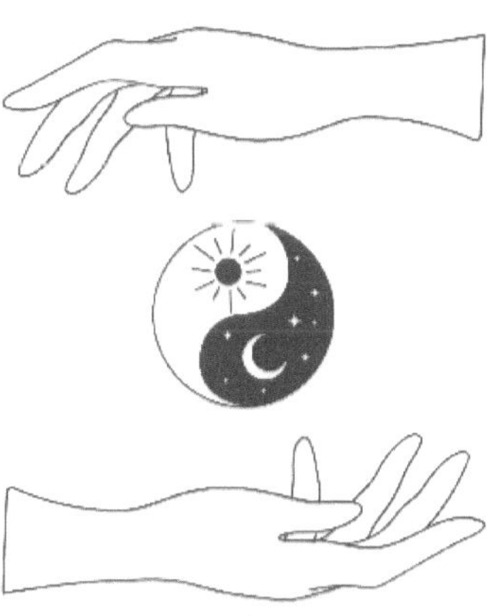

defined by the Oxford English dictionary, is: "*Capacity of judging rightly matters relating to life & conduct; soundness of judgement in the choice of means & ends.*" Wisdom is also defined as the light which dispels darkness.

To grow spiritually & to expand our consciousness, we have to develop wisdom. From the definition of the Oxford Dictionary, we find that it is a soundness of judgement in the choice of the methods & the final results. We can conclude that there is a state which the human being can reach & which allows for correct judgement all the time, allowing us always to choose the right path. Wisdom also assists in making the right decisions. If you imagine that you can reach a state of inner development whereby you consistently make only the right decisions, then there shall be no room for suffering. And all this is achievable by the cultivation of wisdom. In deep meditation, we get access to wisdom. It is also acquired by choosing to be calm all the time- so effectively, it is pure self-control. And to be in perpetual restlessness is the absence of wisdom.

Not all men will possess all of the properties of masculine energy. Some will be surely lacking & must be developed. This is the process of the completion of the male's characteristics. For example, you will need to perform the following tasks: set goals & take decisive actions towards achieving them, develop your problem-solving faculties, practice self-discipline & self-control & cultivate your physical strength and endurance. As you can see, we are all far from being complete as a male itself & the spiritual instruction is to become greater than a fully developed male to become enlightened.

Consciousness of the nature of masculine energy is crucial to the self-development of the individual as well as to the complete development of the maximum potential. But if we live life without depth, we shall never touch down on the appropriate qualities that we need the most & we shall falsely believe "*this is it & there is nothing more to it.*" It is a serious misconception especially when we think that we are a mere mortal human being. In a man, there are both masculine & feminine energies prevailing. And for a man to behave as a man, he has to have more male energies than female energies- however minimal exceptions exist due to inborn traits or subsequent change of mindset towards heterosexuality/or homosexuality. With respect to evolving to higher consciousness, the man then has to develop more feminine characteristics until both are balanced. Such is what happens in terms of the transformation of the inner energies. Balancing masculine & feminine energies brings harmony to life.

Feminine energy is basically related to the emotions of the woman. It is unpredictable, intuitive & related to feelings. A list of feminine energies is as follows: flexibility, receptivity, vulnerability, intuition, empathy, creativity & nurturing. All these qualities may be acquired by meditating, spending time in nature, dancing & sharing feelings. To be flexible means that you are able to make compromises rather than staying rigid. Receptivity is all about being able to sense what is really happening & to be open to new opportunities. A woman is more vulnerable compared to a man & we say vulnerability is feminine by nature. Intuition is the process of joining understanding & feeling together- it is the act of truly knowing without knowing just like a strong gut feeling. Empaths are extremely easy-going & open persons; they can connect with almost everyone & make them feel at ease. They can also readily understand the feelings of others. Creativity is the act of producing something new or a new version of something already existing. It requires a special type of thinking. And lastly, nurturing relates to the supportive nature of feminine energy. It can also be called motherhood.

Just like in a man, the woman possesses both feminine & masculine energies, with the former greater than the latter. Exceptions also exist whereby a woman shows more male behavioural traits. Therefore, for a woman to achieve a balanced & harmonious life, she has to develop the characteristics of masculine energy such as strength, courage, assertiveness, independence, logical reasoning & confidence. When this happens, then there is a perfect balance between the two types of energies. From there now, the potential to rise further & expand the awareness will be easier. Of course, the process is not divided into steps such as I have described- it is rather a global

& integrated process but I wanted to explain in more detail the involvement of masculine & feminine energies in spiritual growth. Everything will happen naturally by all the processes involved in the search for enlightenment- there is no need to become aware of what is happening. Nevertheless, both men & women will feel & know that change has occurred.

From the standpoint of energies, therefore, the serious spiritual aspirant is asked to understand what are the predominant energies & to take corresponding actions. Knowing oneself is not an easy task & will require careful & persistent introspection of one's behaviours. Afterwards, two important steps will be needed. The first one shall be to increase what is lacking & to decrease what is in excess. And the second step is to develop totally new behavioural patterns if they are inexistent. You can guess that it shall definitely not be a simple process & will require steadfast determination but the results are astonishing. Some spiritual scholars have rightly described the act of accessing the divine world as a spiritual war! I believe there is an extent of reality in such a description. On a daily basis, there is a fight going on against emotions, behaviours & the material world in general. But you should not be discouraged as divine support is always available.

On another level, our body is made of the five elements of ether(spirit), fire, water, air & earth. Spirit is the first creation, then comes successively fire, water, air & earth. These elements combine to give us our body & its metabolic functions. For example, if there is no water on our tongue, we shall lose the faculty of taste. And when

we feel hungry, it is the fire of the stomach which is in action. Except for ether or spirit, all these five elements can be classified as either masculine or feminine. Fire is of masculine nature & is associated with life force, strength & activity. It is purifying & used to fight away darkness. Fire produces light & has immense transformative capabilities- meditation is also a fire. Water, the third creation is of feminine nature. When the divine waters are impregnated by spirit, then there is the Big Bang of creation & from the waters, all creations emerge. Water represents our emotions & the unconscious mind. Water has a physical existence & is essential for the functioning of all our senses. Both male & female semen are always of moist nature & water is therefore responsible for reproduction. The next element air is related to our intelligence, new beginnings & creativity. It is a masculine energy. It has no permanent form & serves at a spiritual level to interconnect all creations as we are all permanently in touch with air. Earth as the last of the five elements is feminine energy. It represents stability, fertility, groundedness, maternal energy, materiality & stillness. Earth is the place of birth & death. You will notice that creation is perfectly balanced with spirit at the centre of two masculine & two feminine energies. If there was one more of either masculine or feminine energies, this would be the cause of an imbalance.

Now, men & women are made to live with each other in a relationship to establish a family. Can you see why there exists so many healthy & unhealthy disagreements & tensions in couples? At an energy level, if a man & a woman have unbalanced masculine & feminine energies, then we say both partners are incompatible. Thus, compatibility must first be at the level of internal energies. Afterwards, all other things will be compatible. But nobody teaches us all this fine knowledge about ourselves & our energies. The more we know, the lesser the mistakes & the lesser the sufferings!

Next time, you look around yourself, try to see whether it is a masculine or a feminine energy which is in action, remembering that we all have a percentage of each of them. It is the balance of masculine & feminine energies which fosters harmony in life. And if you think about all the water & air pollution that we are generating every day, then it will be easy to understand the gigantesque impacts on the environment. When the masculine & feminine energies of nature are disturbed by modernisation, then there is an equal rebuff which comes as severe climatic changes & increased intensity of natural catastrophes. Energy cannot be static- it has to flow or be transformed.

Chapter 17

The Mystery of Enlightenment

> *Thinking too much breaks the link with the guidance of the heart. (Chinese Proverb)*

The process of becoming what we were at our origin is called enlightenment. Other terms describing the same process are illumination, awakening, self-realisation, samadhi & rebirth. Very few people are aware of such a process although the number is increasing steadily. For those who are aware of it, there is then a significantly low percentage of persons who want to dedicate time to study & to implement. Enlightenment is a gradual process of liberation from all material bondages & it is not a simple matter to tackle. It requires both self-discipline & support from a learned spiritual master to reach that height of consciousness. The focus of enlightenment is entirely on the expansion of the  awareness of the human being. But how far is the human race conscious that consciousness is evolutive? This forms part of Universal Knowledge which becomes accessible at higher levels of meditation or by the grace of God/or the spiritual master. The majority of people believe that there is nothing to improve with regards to our energy levels & that in any case, we shall die one day- so we better make the most of all the available enjoyments. In spiritual jargon, this is called "**material entanglement**" & "**ignorance**".

Enlightenment is not a topic that is used even in religious gatherings. Or if it is discussed, the subject is touched very lightly because it requires knowledge & experience on the matter to be able to share with the crowd. And this is where the gap lies. Religion in itself has rarely produced enlightened individuals. The process & methodology is only partially available at the level of religion. Most enlightened persons have found the Path outside the scope of religion. I am not against religion but I am just stating the facts based on Universal Knowledge & experience. Religion is certainly the first step to becoming God-conscious but we have to admit that after some time, there is only a repetition of the same rituals year in and year out. For somebody who is looking for newness & answers to deep questions, these answers are found outside the context of religion- they are found in the spiritual realm. For the sake of understanding, religion is focussed on rituals whereas there are absolutely no rituals in spirituality.

When we say that enlightenment is also illumination, then we are automatically inferring that there is the presence of darkness. Again, few of us are conscious of the varieties of darkness which are present in the human body. Another term regularly used for darkness in spiritual discourses is ignorance. Knowledge is the absence of ignorance. Therefore, the more we know, the less ignorant we are & the more illuminated we become. Knowledge is vast but I am here referring to spiritual knowledge, the light which removes a person from the shackles of darknesses. To be in ignorance is a dangerous situation but most people are not aware of its dangers for a human life. We are aware of material dangers such as the effects of viruses, drugs, car accidents, reduced safety at night & when alone, etc. Before

I describe enlightenment further, it is worthwhile to understand what darknesses exist within us. Actually, all negative feelings are darknesses but all of them do not carry the same weight. The worst of all negative feelings is guilt. This feeling, whether validated or unreal generates highly impactful symptoms, which can last a whole lifetime. Next, we have fear, anxiety, paranoia, doubts, hesitation, lack of self-confidence, worry, impatience, restlessness, mistrust, impulsiveness, ignorance, negligence, anger, greed, lust, complacency, pride, attachment, arrogance, unwillingness to learn, grudge, lack of forgiveness, etc. As you can see the list is really long. It would seem we have more darkness than light- this is the bitter truth of the material world. The reason is that our mind, when untrained & conditioned by the material world, is essentially negative. And the mind is such that it does not differentiate between positive & negative thoughts. It Just thinks. Intelligence will perform the discrimination of thoughts. The task now is how we tackle the cleansing of all these impurities which are found in our personal nature. The crux of the matter lies first of all in being truly conscious of our nature- a hard pill to swallow most of the time as the ego will interfere in the process. But, once awareness is present, then it is easier to start cleansing. You will find that it is essentially the control of the mind which must be performed. That is why we say in spiritual classes that *"we are what our mind is"*. It is certainly not a simple task to train the mind, just as is the case for a wild animal. You should not be baited to think that the mind will be tamed in a few months. This will last for several years. Great patience will be the key. Like I always say during motivational speeches, if we can devote four years of life to earn a bachelor's degree in engineering, management, law, etc, I think we can also spend several years to earn a bachelor's in personal development. Society does not think in these terms but I am convinced you have seen the logic. It is a question of being guided by the right authority, the spiritual authority.

Apart from cleansing the mind, we also have to clear our hearts from impure emotions. These are also positive & negative. The more your heart is broken, the more negative as a person you will be. Modern management has discovered that the emotional quotient termed EQ is much more important than the intelligence quotient IQ, to the extent that nowadays, smart recruiters select the high EQ job applicants rather than the high IQ job applicants. Because studies have shown that high EQ employees are better performers. In fact, these high EQ employees are better at handling their emotions & understanding the emotions of colleagues. Hence, they are more productive & don't get disturbed easily. Emotional stability is the backbone of a positive lifestyle. When we get upset by everything, we shall not be able to free ourselves from the chains of the physical world. Emotions create a great imbalance in our internal energy, which we don't perceive but which we externalise through negative reactions such as anger, fear, cries, shouts, hysteria, swearing, etc. In addition, we can also suffer from health issues like breathlessness, fainting, migraine & insomnia. Therefore, emotional control is crucial in self-realisation. And you will be surprised that it is not only negative emotions that must be controlled but the positive ones as well. This is because both make us deviate from our initial state of balance. Most people would tend to believe that they need only to control negative emotions. This phenomenon is called to be undisturbed. Being disturbed is a waste of energy & if we are wasting energy, how shall we ascend to higher levels of consciousness? On the contrary, the method is to conserve energy to increase our personal vibration.

This is easier said than done. Patience, perseverance & resilience are the spiritual qualities that you must develop. You will need to have the perfect reaction to all incoming negativities every day. And the perfect reaction is to have no reaction at all. Slowly when you can do this, the ego will be weakened & will lose

> *You realise therefore that to be enlightened, it is a question of being positive all the time & to remain undisturbed.*

its control over you. The aim is to make the ego so powerless that it stops making us make mistakes in our lives. This is the process of overcoming oneself & that is how you become wise & powerful. But the world teaches us to do all the contrary, that is to show our power by overcoming others!

The overcoming of the ego & hence illumination is greatly helped by meditation, yoga & breathing exercises. Without them, progress will be undermined. All these spiritual practices serve to bring the mind under control. That is why it is only daily practice which will give the desired results. Performing the exercises of yoga, meditation & breathing once a week is just a hobby like practicing a sport. The conditioned mind requires daily training to prevent it from slipping back into its bad habits. As indeed the mind is very fickle & will carry on its own without permission. It is a difficult task to find "**time**" for beneficial activities every day as we let ourselves be trapped by time robbers. They are present & have become our conditioned routine: watching our favourite television series one after the other, surfing on social media, working till late, bringing work home, laziness, etc. This is what is called conditioning- we allow external events to dictate the course of our life. We follow instead of taking the lead. And what do we follow? The world & its proposals for increased & sustained leisure. That is the problem we have on hand; to break that conditioning & dependence to claim our freedom! Unfortunately, very few will attempt to deviate from the normal course of life as it has become an ingrained bad habit- such is the power of the energy of the material world. Uprooting bad habits is the easiest way to progress compared to acquiring new knowledge. I touched on this in a previous chapter when I wrote about learning & unlearning. And it is on the latter that we must concentrate. If you imagine a huge balloon which has heavy sandbags attached to it, you will agree that pumping more gas into it will be less beneficial for it to rise. Only discarding a few sandbags & keeping the same amount of gas will create remarkable results. The same is applicable to the sphere of human development; and the sandbags in our lives are our negativities, bad habits & moodiness. One astonishing higher knowledge is that when you drop your emotions such as vanity, anger, lust, fear & other negative vibrations, then God starts to fill you up with divine energy. Otherwise, there is no space available. This logic is very simple to understand. In addition, positive energies cannot live by side with negative energies.

The act of ascending to higher levels of consciousness is the process of becoming divine. Now, if you inform the common man that he has in him the capability to transcend physical existence, he will most probably laugh at you, out of sheer ignorance. And because that very ignorance is more widespread than knowledge, then those who are numerous temporarily win the battle of discussion. The majority has power, even if it is a vast majority of ignorant people. But the spiritual man has enough internal resources to go on teaching. Sooner or later, the consciousness of the ignorant will change. This is God's promise. It is wise not to agitate those who oppose themselves to higher learning as confirmed in the Bhagavad Gita 17:15, "*One should not speak in a way to agitate others*"; persisting will be greatly counterproductive. It is all a question of divine timing. But certainly, those who are in need of higher knowledge will be benefitted- of this, I am 100% sure. Many good people would wish that God should change all those difficult persons in one go & make life easier on Earth. It does not work this way. We all have our personal state of evolution & we cannot jump the steps of further evolution. Nasty experience is a tremendous teacher if we allow it. God has granted us a certain amount of freedom & we have not used it properly. Many evils are created by ourselves because we tamper with nature & because we forget our spiritual identity.

Most of you believe that enlightenment is "**reserved**" for monks & yogis. I can tell you that this is not the case. We all have inside of us that sacredness which is dormant & needs awakening. Those yogis who have dared to try are the ones who eventually succeed. How can we expect to achieve something if we don't even try? The obstacle lies in personal beliefs & the strength of the material energies. The battle between spiritual & material is indeed not a simple one but rare fruits of spirit grow abundantly on the soil of detachment. Attachment is the opposite of detachment. The instruction from the spiritual masters is to practice detachment to start self-
development. People confuse detachment with a lack of caring. You will be surprised to learn that the greatest potential to love lies in detachment as attachment is a major cause of suffering. To be attached means to become dependent just like two lovers who are very fond of their presence & feel lost or impatient during mutual absence. Our happiness cannot depend upon somebody else as this is a risky business- we must be able to be happy on our own. That is why a breakup is so devastating because there is dependence & addiction just like with drugs. Detachment from people & objects will be a good preparation towards enlightenment. Loneliness is an ingredient that plays a crucial role in self-realisation. So before getting engaged in a

relationship or even marriage, you should sit down with yourself & decide what are your aims in life.

This is not an easy question to answer. As it is simpler to follow the world rather than go against it. There are two options to follow a spiritual life. Either we start early before marriage or we do it after our children have become independent & are settled in their lives. But we have to be conscious of it. If you start a spiritual life early, that does not mean you won't get married! If God wishes so, then He will certainly arrange to make you meet the appropriate partner- and He will never be wrong in the choice.

Chapter 18

Spiritual Experiences

The golden rule of a peaceful life is to adopt tranquillity in disturbance. (Chinese Proverb)

The world of spirituality is indeed a very special one & at the same time, it is full of rewarding & extraordinary personal experiences. In the beginning, there are no experiences at all because the consciousness has not yet expanded sufficiently. Concerning meditation, the practitioner will certainly feel temporary peace & some lightness inside the head. But these will disappear after some hours due to the material energies which are able to overcome the  short-lived achievement. But, this small experience in itself will serve to motivate the meditator to persevere until gradually the effects of meditation will last longer. Nevertheless, we should never start a spiritual life with the sole aim of living extraordinary experiences & for showing off. You will readily find yourself in a difficult situation.

The twice-daily practice of meditation is crucial for spiritual experiences to manifest themselves. In the beginning, it is very common to see beautiful colours which seem to be glowing on the inner black screen of the forehead. These colours will serve as a reinforcement of the willpower to continue meditating- but don't let it become a frenzy for repetition of the experience as it will cause more harm than good. The Universe is the driver behind all meditation sessions & it shall be futile to try to take control- it is always a unidirectional flow. As you gather more experience & mental power, you will be able to "**hold on**" to the magnificent colours & be lost in the contemplation. At this stage, the duration of meditation shall become longer & you should make the necessary efforts to accommodate this in your daily routine. In the presence of such magnificent colours, the notion of time completely changes as what seemed to be a short meditation was in reality way more when you will check the clock! It is literally like transposing to another dimension where time has other characteristics which we have never dealt with.

Apart from colours, the meditator will have visions- they can be of places, people, objects & anything that the Universe decides to show you. It is very common to see a blue sky, trees, flowers, the ocean, people you know & don't know & even saints, deities and much more. Care must be exercised not to confuse imagination with visions. Both can happen & with time, you will notice which were imaginations & which were visions. It is not a mistake to imagine things in meditation- what has to happen in terms of progress will come in its own timing. There is nothing to worry about. Those visions will also leave a tremendous impact on your inner feelings as they are more vivid than dreams. That is why meditation is a very powerful technique to grow spiritually- other measures will also be required & you are already conversant with them now.

Smelling unknown fragrances, vibrations in some areas of the body especially the chakras & feeling of cold or hot currents are also quite common. Very often, the meditator will doubt that such experiences can occur because, in the waking state, such observations will never happen in the way that they happen in deep meditation. Gradually, as there is repetition of the same experiences, then a sense of familiarity & confidence will follow. All these are signs that there is progress in the meditation process, which is so important to develop a stronger faith on the spiritual path. It happens that meditation becomes a mechanical process rather than a serious & esoteric practice- this is when boredom will seep in & eventually will discourage the practitioner. A person on the spiritual path must not commit the mistake of overdoing the meditation process-it must be carefully balanced with some simple material life; otherwise, a feeling of demotivation will settle itself in the process.

Spiritual experiences will also take the form of quicker materialisation of thoughts & wishes. You will notice an accrued collaboration from the Universe to manifest your desires. High levels of energy can be euphoric & the practitioner must take care not to allow himself to get carried away by the powerful enthusiasm which is generated when the consciousness is stronger. You don't need to worry about this as you will become aware of your exaggeration very rapidly- this will happen when you are in deep silence & then you shall proceed by yourself to make the necessary amendments. Many of you are probably viewing videos from social media on "**manifestation**"- it happens only when your frequency of vibration has reached a higher level. Our mind, when it becomes fully trained by the fire of meditation, is capable of performing unbelievably high-level tasks.

Spiritual experiences are very personal & will vary from individual to individual. Sometimes, during meditation, you will feel a strange liquid trickling down your throat. And the taste is like something you have never tasted before. After this experience, when you move out of the meditation, you will still feel the taste in your throat but the most stunning thing is that you shall feel totally different. It is difficult to explain the sensations but if it happens one day, you will clearly feel it. In Kriya, this is explained by the amrita experience. Amrita in Hinduism is called the nectar or elixir of life. When this nectar is produced by the body, it goes firstly into the spine & then into the whole body. The effects are like a rekindling of the vital force of the body.

Another beautiful experience of deep meditation is an out-of-body experience, called OBE. In this situation, the meditator's spirit will move out of the body & shall be able to see himself meditating. With experience, the spirit can wander in the same room or house & later on, may practice visiting other places. This most stunning experience is proof that spirit does exist & that meditation can show the distinction between the body & spirit. OBE is not accepted by science because the scenario cannot be captured on camera but for the practitioner, the experience is real & not a dream. There are similar occurrences which happen in medical institutions whereby patients who have been reported as dead suddenly come back to life after several minutes. These examples have been classified as near-death experiences, NDE. In all cases, the patients have seen themselves hovering over their bodies & some even report going through a tunnel of dazzling white light. And after this experience, the patient's life is no longer the same. This dazzling white light can also be perceived in deep meditation.

Beautiful sounds can also be heard after a long, regular practice: sounds of a distant bell, conch, flute music, waterfall, humming of bees & rumbling of clouds. All these sounds will come by themselves & it is pointless to try to repeat the experience. We don't meditate for the sake of having extraordinary experiences but to transform & become a better human being. Indeed, it can be said that meditation is a world of its own & needs to be mastered step by step. Spiritual ego is something which exists & it relates to people who like to boast about their personal experiences even though they have been instructed to refrain from this. Some people also like to share & compare their experiences- something to be avoided at all costs.

When a person meditates regularly with a high level of self-discipline, there shall be an impact on the relationships. On one hand, all current associations which are for his highest good will be preserved while those which are no more required for him shall be brushed aside- this happens as per the Highest will. On the other hand, all new associations that will be required for his benefit shall be arranged by the divine. As such, a meditator may feel destabilised by the loss of some personal relationships: there is nothing to worry about since meditation is one of the best spiritual tools to deconstruct a person as well as to reconstruct a completely new identity- the spiritual identity. For those who have reached the topmost level, very often, a life of solitude will be adopted & as you will have realised, in this instance, the number of personal & social interactions is a bare minimum & very often it is void. This occurs as the taste for material enjoyment will be completely lost & because the light has overcome the darkness & the spiritual energy has overcome the material energy.

Self-healing is also a direct consequence of high-level meditation. When the frequency of vibration of a practitioner has reached a certain level, then the capacity to heal personal illnesses will be developed. The healing of others shall also be possible as the spiritual energy can be transferred temporarily to a sick person- an illness as explained in an earlier chapter is in reality an imbalance of energy. So, when the initial level of energy is restored, then a healing is produced. Self-healing will also take the form of a greater number of preventive measures in terms of eating habits & other habits. This new lifestyle catalysed by the energy of meditation will then serve to prevent illnesses- that is, It Is the adoption of the healthiest lifestyle.

The most readily observable spiritual experiences are the feelings of peace, lightness & joy. These shall be clearly felt & will even be observable on the face as a peculiar glow. It is said that the face of a person is the mirror image of his internal environment. So, when the inner world has been pacified by prominent self-discipline, then the outer world also shall be rectified. Indeed, it is the inner world which is in control of the outer world. A peaceful person shall never make mistakes as he is in full control of the body & its five senses. Our true nature is that tranquillity which is felt in deep meditation, not the daily states of impatience, rush & restlessness. This is a great illusion & is the actual state in which the modern world forces us to step into. And most of us unconsciously follow the pace & the fashions of the world without much questioning & resistance.

A very particular experience that you will notice at high levels of meditation is that perfect strangers will often inform you that they know you & will even ask where you met them. This is truly a past life reconnection that has happened- the person will be adamant that they know you & you shall also feel that this person is very familiar to you- with the only difference that due to your meditation experience, you will know for sure that you have never met this person in this life, timeline & dimension but certainly in another life, timeline & dimension. It will also happen that small children of two to seven years will be very attracted to you! All this will be happening due to the attraction of the two inner energies. The same phenomenon will be observed with pets & wild animals, who will let you approach them without fear & apprehension of any kind. Animals can readily sense the energies of a person as well as the energies of this world. We have lost this important & beautiful faculty due to a high waste of our energy in material affairs. Animals are more instinctive than we are & instinct is a magnificent tool to tap into the world of the unknown. And most people are afraid of the unknown as the world has conditioned us to know rather than to feel-animals are developed to feel. Do you know why? Because animals don't worry as much as we do. Start to worry less & observe how more intuitive & instinctive you will become.

Chapter 19

The Eternal God & the Other Gods

*When you reach that stage where nothing upsets you,
then you will start to drink the nectar of happiness.*

Many religions have their own Gods & Goddesses- each with a different name. A few religions have only one God. The question which arises is how many Gods are there in reality? In Hinduism, the number is vast & Gods are attributed to each day of the week & even to each planet. And then, we hear about a theory that there is only one God. In the Bhagavad Gita, we read about the existence of demigods. All this literature may confuse the devotee who has not received enough higher knowledge. Some people are very open & they accept the Gods of other religions whereas others are quite closed & don't place any importance on the Gods of other religions. This is a question of behaviour based on beliefs, culture & tradition. It is very important to understand what we mean by God. It would seem that not all of us refer to the same God while it may be that some of us don't even think about who God really is. The debate goes further to a point where some people believe that there is no God & that existence just happened like that, without any "**being**" intervening in the process.

If there were no "**creator**" of the whole Universe, what is the probability that this whole diversity of existence would come up by itself? It is infinitesimally small. If we don't believe in God as a creator, then another important question arises: how does the Universe & all its elements of rotating planets, human & animal complex metabolisms, etc achieve their numerous functions without intelligence? Because this is what makes the creation sustain itself just like the products human beings have created- it's all about intelligence. Then, who has this type of intelligence to perform such a titanic task? If we create using our intelligence, then why is it unreasonable to believe that there is a higher intelligence who is behind everything we see? This is yet again ignorance & ego in action.

The battle between science & spirituality will go on for a very long time as these are two distinctive & completely incompatible elements of our lives. I had the opportunity to be exposed to both of them, in the first instance as a mechanical engineer and then as a spiritual master. With all the spiritual experience that I have gathered, it is impossible for me to believe that God doesn't exist- it's a very strong feeling coupled with extraordinary experiences. From all the healings & predictions that I have made over the years, this is a confirmation that higher levels of consciousness do exist & that without the help of God, such realisations are not possible. I can assure you that I am not the same person that I was fifteen years ago. So, if we can expand our consciousness by careful discipline, what happens at the highest point of consciousness? As you can see, there is a logic in the spiritual process. We need to make an effort to understand that logic & not adopt a one-sided opinion. Experience is a great teacher but for the sake of gathering experience, we have to be open to new Ideas & concepts. Then, we shall be able to decide by ourselves in what to believe.

The modern world needs proof to believe- if a person starts to make miracles, then the chances of believing in divine interventions & the existence of God increase. Even with miracles, a lot of people will still doubt. Believing is both a simple & a very complex behaviour. There is nobody to blame if there is a denial of faith. Our era itself is such an era where the distance between the divine world & our world is the greatest. This has already been predicted by several religions. Spirituality is based on self-discipline & faith- unfortunately, both cannot be measured by any scientific apparatus. But the progress made can indeed be clearly felt. You will know you are different; you will feel it both on the interior & exterior. And you will have a double confirmation when people around you will tell you "*You have changed*!" And if God does not intervene to guide you on the Path & to provide you with the support that is needed, then how do all these positive transformations occur? Because all the methods & prayers that are practiced have been gracefully given to us either directly or by a spiritual master. And all these practices are divine.

Spiritual energy has unfathomable capacities. Science does agree that energy can only be transformed but never created nor destroyed be it kinetic, potential, nuclear & electrical energies. Then, how do we tally this finding with the energy of a human being? With the energy of the Sun & planets? Energy is the basis of all creations not physical matter. The latter arises from the former & not the contrary. Scientific research has proven that the origin of the Universe was a Big Bang. Spiritually, this information already existed in sacred literature several thousands of years ago. Now to manipulate energy transformations, intelligence is required- energy cannot transform by itself into matter without guiding instructions! A brain & a mind to think are also required. Then, who is that master brain & mastermind behind the Big Bang? If we begin to understand that the whole Universe is a transformation of the spiritual energy of God into physical matter, then there is no proof to be given. If we are convinced that there is only intelligence at work all around us like in the photosynthesis of a tree's leaves, in the imperceptible rotation of the Earth, in the ocean tides created by the Moon, in the overcoming of Earth's gravity by a mere colourful butterfly, in the three hundred years lifespan of a tortoise and so on, then it has been truly said in all religions that God is omnipresent as He is that very intelligence which is everywhere. I am fully convinced of this. Furthermore, it is also stated in sacred texts that this one God is invisible, has no shape, has no beginning & no end, and has no birth & death. Then based on this writing found in the Vedas, we can conclude that God exists as the most intelligent energy.

With regard to energy, I would like to highlight that we are essentially energy rather than bones & flesh. All our emotions are energetic in nature as well as our thoughts. Love, joy, fear, anger, greed, excitation, calmness, youth, old age, health & disease are all states of energy. The food & drinks that we consume provide us with the necessary energy to carry out our daily tasks. The calorific value or energetic value of all foods has already been calculated by science. The Earth has magnetic energy associated with it- the North Pole & the South Pole acting as the two magnetic nodes. This also means we are bathed in that magnetic energy every day. With respect to all non-living matter, all these are also energy in its dense form. Because all matter is made of packets of atoms & molecules: the smallest, indivisible representative of matter. Now atoms, molecules & electrons are so microscopic that they have no physical attributes, but they are the essential building blocks of all matter: physical, liquid & vapour. Therefore, matter in its simplest form is made up of atomic energy. You are probably not aware but scientific research has discovered that atoms & molecules can be further subdivided into smaller particles! This means we are getting closer to the exact nature of materials. How you must view energy is that life is His superior energy whereas material energy is His inferior energy.

When there was no creation, there was nothing but emptiness, not darkness. The latter means the absence of light but before creation, light was not yet generated. That emptiness is the origin & source of everything. When the one God started creating, first of all, a self was made so that a recognition was possible- we call this the Higher Self or Universal Spirit. As soon as the Higher Self came into being, the words "**I am**" were pronounced. Because now, non-being(emptiness) is a self-conscious being. I now reveal to you the name of the one God: He is called **I AM THAT I AM**. This God is the manifested God created from the unmanifested origin of all creation & resides in our hearts. Now, the characteristic of spirit whether Universal or Holy or human has a basic function: it generates desires & materialises those desires. Of course, the capability of a divine spirit is monumental compared to the human spirit. Then the Universal Spirit started to create. The first element which was created was fire when the unmanifested thought of having a self; a thought has the attribute of fire. The second created element is water. In this water is now dormant all remaining creations. To liberate the creations in water, the Universal Spirit impregnates the waters & they start boiling creating a big mass of golden colour, called the egg of the Universe- this is the Big Bang that science refers to. It is the gigantic & powerful reaction between the spiritual fire & the spiritual waters which releases the material world. And creation lasted for one whole year- not a human year but a divine year. This explains the sacredness & huge importance of fire & water in many religions. In Hinduism, water is offered to God & different oblations are also offered in fire. In Christianism, the fire of the candle is offered to the Father, Lord Jesus & Mother Mary. And also, water is used for the important ceremony of baptisation. Now creation is alive & going on as per the plan of the Eternal God. Everything in this material world has a start & an end- which we call a lifespan. It varies from a few days to several years in the physical material world & goes up to billions of years in the spiritual world. Then logically, the Universe has its lifetime. The **I AM THAT I AM** presence is not an active presence- He only observes & does not interfere with our freedom. Through spiritual practices, we can make the **I AM THAT I AM** presence active again. Then He will act on our behalf just like Lord Krishna drove the chariot of Arjuna in the Mahabharata some 5100 B.C. The symbolism here is that we should stop driving our life & instead surrender ourselves completely to the divine for complete guidance. Surrendering is not an easy task but with perseverance, it will surely happen. The ego is the unconscious driver of the entire human race because it is the subconscious which predominates rather than pure consciousness. Our subconscious mind distorts reality & is one of our main enemies over & above greed, lust & anger. What is repressed & stored in the subconscious mind is what makes most of our reality. This boils down to the conclusion that our real consciousness is dormant & has to be freed, discovered & awakened by spiritual practices. Unconsciousness or ignorance is in fact the greatest of all sufferings, not stress as modern writers stipulate. To be ignorant & not know that one is ignorant is a great danger. It will create its reality as a shield over the already existing genuine reality. This is called, in spiritual matters, the illusion of the material world. In Hindu terms, it is called "**maya**".

Before ending this chapter, I wanted to clear a misunderstanding as well as an injustice to women. When referring to God, you will find in all literature that we use the pronoun "**HE**". This is an aberration in the sense that it is a kind of discrimination to the feminine gender. In truth, God is both male & female- otherwise, it would be impossible for him to create the feminine counterparts of all creations. We can certainly pray to God by referring to him as our Father God or Mother God: both will yield the same results. But the trend which society has taken over the centuries is that it tends to be male-dominated. There are encouraging signs of efforts to catch up in several domains. Nevertheless, the idea of trying to make men & women equal is rather daunting because both are here to complement each other, not to compete. Truly, for a man to complete his character, he has to develop his feminine internal attributes & likewise, a woman must develop her innate masculine attributes to become complete. That is to say, a fully developed person has the right balance of both masculine & feminine energies.

Chapter 20

About Death

> *Spirituality is not a way to avoid punishment or to think about right & wrong. It is allowing guidance by life.*
> *(Chinese Proverb)*

One of the greatest of all ignorance is the absence of knowledge about death. So many beliefs exist on this weird phenomenon which causes so much dismay in a person's life. It is also surrounded by a lot of superstitions of which we don't even know the origin & explanations. When death strikes a family, it creates a whirlpool of negative emotions which the common man is unable to handle. Sadness & grief are deep & overwhelming in such an occurrence as we don't accept separation from a family member. In some

cases, death causes a profound mental shock which lasts for several years or even a whole lifetime. The problem is we are not prepared for such a happening. Very few adults have the necessary higher knowledge about the reality of death. Religious institutions do share their knowledge on death but no efforts are made to absorb the essence of this knowledge- that is why the suffering is intense when it happens. Death can be according to the destined timing or premature- both happen without our knowing. Only learned persons will know.

As soon as there is birth, death is going undoubtedly to happen one day as the physical body is temporary. Physical bodies have the least span of life whereas spiritual bodies have the greatest spans of life. The reason for this is that the frequency of vibration & the purity is much greater for spiritual bodies. Most people view death as negative & disruptive. It certainly is when we are not prepared & don't have enough real information on it. There is always duality in the world. Positive & negative aspects are intertwined closely in everything- it will depend on which angle we look at the person or situation. Then what could be the positive aspects of death? In Hindu religion, there is even a God attributed to death & his name is Yama. It is believed that he comes to take the soul of the deceased person.

Death when viewed positively is a liberation from the body- that very body which is the cause of all our miseries. Taking birth on Earth is absolutely not a blessing as it is the lowest in the ranking of all the existing material planets. We "**fall**" on Earth to pay our karmic debts & to suffer. Whether we are rich or poor, there is nobody who is free from suffering across the globe. There has to be suffering whatever your title, your salary, your possessions, etc. So, this Earth is for suffering. Then, death will be a liberation from all those sufferings. Indeed, it is not necessarily always the case. Because when we die, it's not the end! At death, we are all spirits & souls. And the conditioned & impure soul is always wishing to enter a mated sperm & ovule. Millions of such souls are fighting every day to get back to Earth. The next life & the next body of the soul will depend on the karma which the person has accumulated over all his past lives & the recent previous life. The consciousness at the time of death is crucial in determining the next birth.

That is why both life & death are to be given the greatest attention as we have the power to change our destiny in this human form of life. There are specifically 8,400,000 types of bodies (Bhagavad Gita 8:3) available in the Universe in which a soul can dwell & it encompasses the human, animal & plant realms. Thus, a human life is not always guaranteed after death! Transmigration of the soul to the animal world will happen when we eat a lot of meat & also when we have extremely rude behaviours. Laziness & ignorance will also contribute to being born in the animal & plant worlds because plants have limited mobility just like animals like the bear which hibernate for six months. There are three types of human nature: divine, human & evil. Throughout our life, we accumulate knowledge & develop a certain type of consciousness. These two decide our next birth.

Since we can transmigrate to any type of body after death, then this death is indeed not a death but simply the end of a phase & the start of another phase. This leads to the fact that there are two types of death, one is temporary & the other is final. It is the final death which is the liberation from the body and the greater the sufferings, the greater the potential for greater liberation. Therefore, tiny sufferings will not endow an individual with the release from birth & death- then we can conclude that sometimes a major suffering can also be a blessing. This is another clear example of the dual nature of life. After the final death, there is no other birth- the

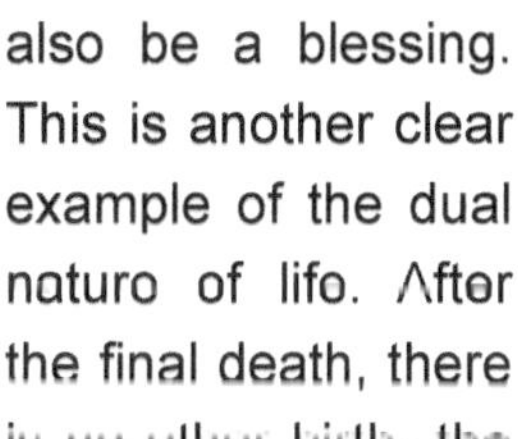

cycle of birth & death is stopped. This is the aim of human life on Earth. We don't come on Earth to enjoy life! This is another illusion on Earth. So, remember at some times, you can be the enjoyer & at others, you shall be enjoyed by people, your body & this life itself. This is not exclusively in sexual terms but in many other different ways such as: when you are cheated, when you are sick, when you lose your job or family member & so on. Ancient sages have rightfully described this Earth as the shackles of sexual life & if you look closer, you will find that this is the case; furthermore, we have its confirmation in Bhagavad Gita 3:39, "*In the material world, the centre of all activities is sex.*" We are not taught what is the aim of a human life. We live life without purpose, without depth & without meaning. This is very superficial & we spend a whole lifetime in ignorance. I was in this situation myself for a very long time, living a life which is not mine but dictated by society. But I kept asking questions to understand the mysteries of life. And life started to answer. That is how I discovered many realities & had so many magnificent experiences in the spiritual world.

It is not a fault to enjoy life but we should exercise care not to exaggerate & not to be attached to enjoyment & to material arrangements. Detachment is opposed to attachment, not to enjoyment. It will take you a while to understand & apply the wisdom of this spiritual statement. Once you get it, your life will be simpler & peaceful. There is another type of death which exists & which does not involve the dissolution of the body. It is the number of times we learn the hard lessons of life. In such cases, we lose some part of ourselves by acquiring & implementing a new paradigm of life. Because we have transformed into a new person just like a snake shedding its old skin to make place for the new skin, likewise, we also become new as we leave the "**old**" behind. This can also be interpreted as a kind of death since the "**old**" us has been killed & replaced by a new "**us**". This is the spiritual process of ascension to achieve enlightenment- we must die several times before our final death. When you die several times like this on the spiritual path, you shall also witness your transformation. You will clearly feel you are no longer the same person. Your reactions, your attitude, your way of life & every other aspect of life will be improved. That is the power of God when He decides to accept you to be transformed & that you also accept to play your part.

So, should we be afraid of death? Should we prepare ourselves for the final death? The answers are obvious. It is a question of belief. We must learn to die intelligently, otherwise we shall get reborn. The Universal Knowledge dictating the rule of death is that whatever you cherish at the time of death, just before your soul leaves your body, that state of life you will unfailingly achieve the next life, stipulated by the Bhagavad Gita 7:23. If you cherish your loved ones, your job, your possessions, you have great chances of coming back to Earth. If you cherish the demigods you worship, you will go to the planets of those demigods. If you cherish the spirits, you have been praying, you shall go to the planet of spirits. And if you cherish the Eternal God, you will be free from the cycle of birth & death. Now, you are probably thinking, let me have fun throughout my life & then during the last few seconds, I shall remember God & make it nevertheless to His kingdom. This will simply not happen as whatever you do as primary activities in your life is impregnated deeply in your consciousness & that is what you will recall at the time of death. Those things of which you are more conscious will come to your mind during the last few seconds: that's the way it works. Therefore, we must learn how to die intelligently- surely a strange idea to grasp & implement, but believe me it is worthwhile to ponder on it. Like I said earlier, you can start a spiritual lie after your children are settled- it's never too late & better late than never! Once we start to add spiritual purpose & meaning to our life, things will definitely turn in a different direction, provided we have the right guidance & simultaneously there is a good level of perseverance. As it happens, science is the study of secondary causes & it does that well, but the study of primary causes is only achieved by wisdom. Death cannot be explained rationally except by making the statement "**life has been lost**", whether it is human, animal or plant life. We need to understand deeply the fundamentals of life & death. Because we are born & we shall die. Just like you have a car or laptop, you need to know the basics of its effective operations & some troubleshooting. Then, when you are stuck, you seek professional advice & support. I want you to understand it works the same way with life. We know fairly well how to live, how to answer simple questions & how to tackle minor issues. But when confronted with complex issues, we also have to seek expert advice & guidance. But many times, we stop at complex problems & don't probe deep enough for solutions because of reduced willpower. Because maybe your illness & innumerable visits to the doctor are a karmic reaction which shall never be solved by any branch of specialised medicine. You should knock open several doors before giving up. I can assure you that willpower is nothing but the presence & support of God in your life. It comes from within & should be developed since early adulthood because if we have strong willpower, what or who will stop us? Nobody & nothing! We are what our mind is. Always remember this. You have the innate power to carve your destiny & to even overcome death. Of that, I am 100% sure but you limit yourself by reducing the capacity of your mind. Be brave & fight for what you want. Of course, you should run after morally & ethically acceptable things.

Another thing to know about death is what happens in the event of a premature death. This may happen for several reasons like an accident, foul play or medical negligence and so on. In such a situation, the spirit of the person will stay on Earth and will wander until its karmic time to leave Earth arrives. We call such a spirit a "**tramp soul.**" Some people are sensitive enough to feel the presence of such souls or some even see them depending on the psychic ability they have developed. It can be clairvoyance (to see) or clairaudience (to hear) or clairsentience (to feel). These phenomena exist but care must be exercised as in this area, there are also charlatans who work to cheat.

There is another aspect of death & life which needs to be understood is that through the practice of advanced spiritual exercises, you can increase the duration of your life span by many years. It is famous in India that a few yogis, living as hidden hermits, have reached over two hundred years of age. This is called mysticism & is difficult to explain by logic & scientific experiment. It is a fact & also a spiritual belief. Some would call it a miracle as it cannot be explained by any rational method. But we do know from religious texts that saints & other elevated souls are capable of feats ordinary people cannot perform. Shirdi Sai Baba of India, St Francois of Assisi and Mother Theressa just to name a few were among those saints- they could do miracles as they have become true devotees of God. At this point, we can make the difference between a real devotee & a common devotee. The latter is numerous & forms the majority of all religious followers. The former is rarer & belongs to the spiritual realm. And with regards to death, those who have become a true devotee, God grants them a great gift- that of choosing the way & the date of dying. *"If the yogi is perfect, then he can select the time & situation for leaving this material world."* (Bhagavad Gita 8:23)

Chapter 21

What is the Path (To Heaven)

> *Let it be known if I have created padlocks on this Earth,*
> *then be sure I have also created the keys.*
> *(Lord Krishna)*

In all religions, the aspect of Heaven is thoroughly discussed. And what is sad, is that our religious scholars do not take enough time to explain exactly what Heaven is. But all devotees accept this belief as it is always the case until a Guru (Spiritual Master) comes into your life & starts to slowly show you the Truth in all matters of life.

Religion is going through a major loss of value not because it no longer has its original strength but simply because the power of modernism & material life is increasing at a phenomenal rate. And very few people seem to be conscious of the attachment to material life & all its drawbacks. Now, I am not fully against material life because as soon as we get a physical body on Earth, we have to bear some percentage of materialism - but it has to be a strict minimum just to balance the aspect of spiritual life.

So, what is this Path (to Heaven) that is mentioned to earnest spiritual seekers by the genuine Gurus? Note I mention here genuine Gurus as obviously the charlatan Gurus, unfortunately, exist in this material world. The genuine Guru comes from a disciplic succession which is transmitted through ages from Spiritual Master to Spiritual Master. And the first spiritual master is the one who has received direct initiation & training from God himself. This is discussed in the Bhagavad Gita when Lord Krishna is speaking to Arjuna on the battlefield. In truth, Heaven is not a physical place that we can think of, where everything is perfect. This whole Universe operates in duality, meaning that everything that has been created has its opposite: just like we have love & hate, light & darkness, kindness & rudeness. This would eventually lead us to believe that there is also a Hell.

The Path can be imagined as an invisible link which enables the connection with an infinite source of Light & Love which has the capabilities to help us in all aspects of our lives. That link is the ultimate search of all serious spiritual aspirants & the sole objective of a human life. If we do not adopt this search as the basis of our life, it is not a problem. But given that we live in a world of cause & effect, that is there are reactions to our actions (Even Isaac Newton discovered this Law), the consequence of not choosing to find the Path is repeated births & deaths. Now, after death, it is not a steadfast rule that one shall always beget a human body. There are 8,400,000 types of bodies available in the Universe as stated in the Bhagavad Gita. That includes bodies in the human, animal & plant worlds.

So, what is this source of Light & Love to which we can connect? We call him God, the Almighty, The One God, The Creator of All That is. And together with God, there are his/her assistants in the divine world who act on his behalf: we have archangels, guardian angels, Spiritual Masters, our ancestors & some animal spirits. All these divine helpers get in touch with the spiritual aspirants in many ways & send codes which have to be deciphered. As unbelievable as this may sound, I can guarantee the link DOES exist & I am currently witnessing it. Of course, this connection is not an easy task to perform - it will require years & years of practice in a particular way of life. It also comes in several stages & when one succeeds in passing one stage, one gets access to the next stage, just like the levels in a video game. Discipline, patience, trust & determination are examples of qualities that must be developed in order to be successful.

The quest for the Path can be viewed as a spiritual class to which one has enrolled & there are tests & examinations which one must pass. The higher the levels, the greater the tests, but one is always accompanied & guided by the spiritual world when one is a serious student. Therefore, who is this serious student? It is simply the one who carefully treads on the Path & makes sure that all spiritual instructions are rigorously followed. As you are probably rightly guessing, there are formidable obstacles on the Path, which take the form of temptations, wrong attitudes, not getting up to start over again when fallen and many others. But the result of such great labour cannot be described in words. Just as Lord Jesus states in the Bible, Matthew 9:37: *"The harvest is great; the labourers are few."* So, this is what Lord Jesus meant to say, that the harvest exists & is bountiful & surely there is a way or Path to get access to this harvest & it is only by working as hard as a labourer.

Working hard in this modern world is becoming more & more tedious for the simple reason that all technological developments are aiming at mainly giving us a comfortable life. But does a labourer enjoy a comfortable life? This is the exact diametrical opposition of the modern world with a spiritual world, which poses a real problem & certainly poses the problematic issue of a decision: do I live materially or spiritually? And the majority will decide to enjoy a material life.

Now, in itself, this is not a wrong decision but when we start to see that despite having a successful career, a great house & car, a beautiful family, and yearly trips to foreign lands, one still is not able to achieve peace, tranquillity, happiness, lightness & solutions to all our physical, emotional & mental troubles. But, once on the Path, one is guaranteed to achieve all this provided one believes & works hard.

The Path is not a straight line & the concept of a destination also does not exist since we are talking more of a radical inner transformation. The arrival is a completely renewed state whereby we can really define it as the so-much-written rebirth & awakening or even enlightenment. Truly speaking, the Path may be described as a spiral which takes us repeatedly to the same experiences but at different periods of time, until we have learnt the lessons & mastered how to tackle with precision the same scenario. For example, if one has not yet mastered being calm in the face of adversity, then life will definitely ensure that one faces enough adverse situations to be able to practice! It is so simple & logical when you come to know about it, but so confusing & complex when you are not aware of what is going on in your life! Such is the power of spiritual knowledge also known as Universal Knowledge.

Therefore, what I can guarantee the readers is that the heaven we usually refer to is surely not a physical outer location but an interior space both in your mind & in your heart. So, what does one feel when one is in Heaven? It is twenty-four hours of calmness, humility, joy, zero anger, always willing to help, ever smiling, treating all equally, loving all (humans, animals, plants), success in all one does, simple meals, disconnected with the outer world, simple non-materialistic life. However, material pleasures will not be present in large amounts - one will get sufficient of what one needs. All these qualities are either transmitted by the divine to the serious student or developed by the student over years of disciplined practices. This all seems to be a fairy tale or political promises which are not fulfilled. But, believe me, this is exactly what the divine world & the Universe promise to all serious spiritual aspirants. Human beings can trick you in many ways by luring promises but this never happens with the divine world – it is always willing to lend a helping hand in all areas of your life, provided you do your part. And the rest, it will complete. This is the wonderful experience I have had for the past ten years. When the Universe becomes your best friend, your life is the best. When you are perfectly aligned with the divine world, then there is absolutely nothing to worry about. Your will shall become God's will. And when the individual will & the divine will are one & the same, then manifestation happens.

Alignment with the divine world or Universe is the essential part of walking on the Path. It is like a manual of procedures which you have to follow rigorously, except that the manual does not exist. All the instructions come one after the other & one shall never be able to guess the next steps. And the main driver of the spiritual journey is change. Conversely, it is the resistance to accept changes in one's life which is the greatest of all obstacles. That is why the process of rebirth or awakening or enlightenment is a long & demanding process.

Now, the modern man is neither ready nor prepared to believe & accept that a spiritual link exists. The reason is that the empirical, logical mind of the modern world is based on believing in solid proofs only or with experiments which can be repeated to get the same results every time; whereas, the spiritual & religious dogmas teach us that we must train our minds to believe with faith. In fact, to be precise, the link has always existed because, in Creation, we are God's image. This spiritual knowledge has two main serious connotations. The first one is that we are a sacred being at source! And our sacredness & divinity get spoiled by material life on Earth; we become impure. The second connotation is that the link has always existed since day one, but the connection is blocked as we use our minds improperly due to our freedom of speech, thoughts & actions. Therefore, the available connection is lost.

In itself, this is great news! Because one does not have to re-establish a connection. The primary task at hand is to unclog the pipeline of communication. And God is so loving (my eyes get filled with tears as I type this) that He will help to unclog this pipeline. That is what He is earnestly waiting for... that all His children come back to Him. I am still emotional as I type the last lines of this chapter but I regain my poise as God is in control of my life. And as soon as I think I must control myself, it just happens.

Truly speaking, God is not absent from our lives as I often hear people say this, especially when they are in deep trouble - we move away from him due to our ignorance of spiritual matters. And yet, He is in everybody's heart centre, observing silently & waiting patiently for everyone to make Him active again. This is a clear picture of the task that must be carried out on the Path. Hopefully, now, you have a fair idea of what a spiritual Path can be.

Chapter 22

The Aim of Life is to Connect with God

> *The tortoise inhales three times per minute & lives for around three hundred years; a human being inhales ten to twelve times per minute & lives around eighty years.*

In the beginning, I placed my faith in the human system of life. I have also trusted a few persons in my personal life & professional life. Some people have been of great support both personally & professionally. But when several persons impacted my life negatively, I was greatly disturbed & decided that I must find a way to understand all these mysteries & to delve deeply to seek a solution to the problems of life. It just could not go on this way every year. When I look backwards (which I very rarely do these days), I clearly see how caught up & desperate I was- as if darkness was a part of my life. It took a lot of research, questioning, patience & perseverance to get out of the clutches of the material world. And without divine support, it would have been impossible. When faith has become as solid as a rock, then there is nothing to worry. And that is what you should target for amidst all the difficulties you are going through.

Now I live daily in the remembrance of my loving Father. I cannot live without Him, without praying, without meditating.

Each moment I do my best to see Him in action. Because this is what He asks us to do. To always remember Him. And He never forgets his true devotees. Your close & loved ones may stop giving you support but He will never leave you once He lives in your heart. In the beginning of the search, He may take some time to respond but when He is convinced that you are extremely serious about your spiritual quest, then He comes every time you call for help. Then what else do you need? You see, the development of trust & faith is a long process just like the slow transformation of graphite into diamond- spiritually, we call this the cooking time. I love this term! And instantaneous cooking does not exist. But the modern world likes to offer us quick & almost instantaneous gratifications- we get used to this & our expectations for more ready-made products & instantaneous gratifications become huge. Research keeps going on how to improve & facilitate our lives but what the modern world is unaware of is that the more facilities we have, the weaker our willpower & our mind. Now, let me inform you that the Universal Cooker of this Universe is called time. We are all cooked at different temperatures for different periods of time.

Therefore, the spiritual cooking of a true devotee also takes its time. The more you are impatient, the more the chances of quitting. You have no chance to accelerate the process by using your intelligence- the divine world which is in control of the process will simply turn you down. I tried a few times to go quickly but the setbacks I received each time were enough to learn the lesson. But failing is also part of learning! As you can see, there is nothing to worry about except if you are not playing your part properly. Success happens in its divine timing. You only have to believe & do your part steadily & with utmost discipline. It is indeed a great life to live in the physical world but with the mind focussed on the spiritual world. If your mind is always on the material world, you will always suffer. The only way to break the alternate cycles of pain & pleasure is to adopt a spiritual way of life. I have tried to be happy with great jobs, great salaries, and to work abroad but there was always something missing. That missing link is the connection with God. Once you re-establish the link, you will always be on top of all the waves of life. This is guaranteed. Whatever waves may come, you shall always keep your balance. But you must work very hard for that. If it is possible to study hard at college or university for so many years, why should it be difficult to spend several years in search of God?

What makes it difficult to turn to God? It is due to the numerous temptations & pleasures that are available. In the old days, I would leave God aside & stay awake to watch a Manchester United football game or spend four to five hours watching a tennis final between anyone of Roger Federer or Novak Djokovic or Rafael Nadal! Can you imagine that? It's almost half a day. Now, it's God first. That is the willpower you must develop. I haven't quit the love for sports either because I am a spiritual person. I record and watch little by little every day. You know what? God is extremely pleased when you do that. He sees you are putting Him first- that is what must be done. Always Him first. And when the supporter of this whole Universe is pleased with you, then He will start to please you. Your mind will always trick you to forget God. You will need to exercise great diligence in the control of the mind. If ever you believe the spiritual world is tough to apprehend, then use only this principle: "*The cultivation of the Higher Self is the rectification of the mind.*"

Once you appreciate that it is your mind which is pulling you down, then you have been able to steer the compass of your life towards the North Pole of spirituality. In the Vedas, we are informed that the cause of being reborn is conduct. Karma is the phenomenon which measures our conduct & which therefore conditions our next birth. And conduct is based on our thoughts, which originate from our mind. So, the control of the mind will lead to better conduct, then better karma & a better life next birth. The sequence is logical. Still better, is to have perfect control of the mind which will lead to perfect conduct & a breakage of the cycle of birth & death. Just take a look around you in your house, your social media account, your neighbourhood or the news bulletins, you will see how far we are from perfect conduct be it for the common man, the educated man, the businessman & the politicians. Unfortunately, the majority of people have little control over their minds. This is the tragedy on Earth. On top of that, few of us are aware that our minds are essentially negative as proven by research. You will here realise that the process of ending repeated birth is simply by being extra cautious of your behaviour- it does not relate to which religion you belong, which festivals you celebrate, how many times you fast in a week, etc. It's just plain, correct, morally acceptable behaviours.

Reconnecting with God is the purpose of our life because we need to get out of the illusion that we are a body made of flesh & bones. And that we are made up of emotions & feelings which swing up & down like a yoyo throughout all our life. We are sacred! We are made in the image of God. We can discover all the godlike qualities & start to inculcate them in our routine. This is the divine demand & not the submission to all kinds of pleasures. When the soul & the mind are still attached to the body & its five senses, then we are lost. Because it is the senses which are the drivers of the chariot of your life, not your true self. The senses will always tempt you to utilize them in all possible ways & in any repeated quantity. But have you ever been satisfied by any excess amount of eating delicious foods, playing lotteries, placing bets, sexual intercourse, travelling, resting, working, shopping, etc? Some time afterwards, your cravings flare up again & the cycle continues. This is because material desires are like fires you cannot extinguish. And the more you quench your material appetites, the more often the desires come back to haunt you & ask you to give in again- it's more, more & more! And surely you give in as your mind is weak. That is the basis of material life. In the quest for God, you will learn to be satisfied with little & simple things. If you are still exaggerating in your demands, then you are still invisibly caught up in the material world. "**Less is more**" - this is the paradigm of the spiritual world.

You don't have to travel to famous sacred places to find God. He is everywhere. He is right there with you, lying deactivated in your heart. You have to activate Him! It is customary to travel to spiritual places in groups or alone to satisfy the traditions. I don't believe in this anymore. I have also stopped celebrating almost all Hindu festivals as they don't stir up any emotions in my heart anymore. Meditating for thirty minutes gives me great peace which I will not find by driving thirty minutes to a religious place, praying there & driving back home for another thirty minutes. In all, it's almost one & a half hours used up with little results whereas in thirty minutes, I have had a beautiful experience. I trust more to be cautious about my conduct rather than be fearful because I am not celebrating religiously. This is another illusion in this world- to follow the crowd. What if the crowd is ignorant? I am not against going to church & temple but I want to emphasize that there are greater & more subtle experiences of God in the spiritual practice.

There is a great mistake made by many spiritual aspirants; it is that they believe they must know God, who God is & what God does, etc. You shall never know this by any practice because where the source of everything is, the human mind cannot reach there by any level of heightened consciousness. That is the very place where God is sending his eternal light across the whole Universe. Science has shown that this Universe & all its components are precisely moving slowly but surely towards a focal point situated very far away in the distant Universe. I can safely tell you that this point of convergence is where God is to be found. At the time of the dissolution of the Universe, everything goes back into God, stays dormant for some time & is then released into creation again. And the cycle continues- creation & dissolution. The point is not to know & understand God but to follow His principles. And most important is to love God. Loving God will make Him love you back. And what does a loving father do to his children? He blesses them with gifts. If you love to get gifts, then start today to love God. He shall bestow upon you both spiritual & material gifts.

How do we love God? It is just the way you love a person. When you love someone truly & a lot, you spend a lot of time together on the phone, eating together, and going places together, the person is always on your mind & on your lips and so on. Likewise, to love God, you must spend time with Him, pray to Him with joy & devotion (not casually & forcefully), and think of Him regularly, e.g. when eating, driving, surfing on the internet, singing devotional song, doing all your tasks in the name of God. Above all, always be thankful a lot of times every day for all you feel God has done for you. In this way, when you remember Him, then He will also remember you. You cannot be selfish & pray only during difficult moments- this tendency will not make Him compassionate towards you. Avoid using the term "**must**" as in the saying *"I must go to pray."* Just say *"it is time for me to pray."* "**Must**" implies obligation & does not come from the heart. We should never pray half-heartedly! It is then compulsion, not love. Many times, rituals are done by obligation or by procedural/ traditional implications. God is moved by acts of love.

Adoration is a higher form of love. In this case, the love for God has reached a higher stage. You will feel the love of God when you pray, you will know what to do & what not, you will feel calm & peaceful, you will not rush every day to do your tasks, you will believe more in yourself, you shall be kind & generous to yourself & to others. When God is in your life, He will never leave you, and even you won't be able to leave Him. It is the greatest of all partnerships. Everyone of you can achieve this level of spiritual awareness- you must work hard for it. If you believe life is meant to sleep, wake up, go to work, come back home, eat, watch television & social media, have some outings during the weekends, and look after your family, then you are stuck in the whirlpool of material life. Your primary duty is to love God, to pray fervently, to be helpful to others, to be aware of your highest aim in life & to know why you are born as a human being. All these answers I have obtained, trusted & implemented in my life. And it is a great experience after a long journey of learning, discovery, unlearning, fighting with oneself, falling down, doubting & much more. I sincerely encourage you to start & believe that you can do it. I will not say it is an easy decision & an easy path to follow. But I can say it is worthwhile. May God bless all of you with love & light.